WILDERNESS GEAR
YOU CAN MAKE YOURSELF

OTHER BOOKS BY BRADFORD ANGIER

At Home in the Woods

How to Build Your Home in the Woods

The Ghost of Spirit River

A Star to the North

The Home Medical Handbook

Living Off the Country / How to Stay Alive in the Woods

On Your Own in the Wilderness

How to Go Live in the Woods on $10 a Week

Wilderness Cookery

We Like It Wild

Home in Your Pack

Free for the Eating

More Free-for-the-Eating Wild Foods

Skills for Taming the Wilds

Being Your Own Wilderness Doctor

The Art and Science of Taking to the Woods

Introduction to Canoeing

How to Live in the Woods on Pennies a Day

Gourmet Cooking for Free / Food-from-the-Woods Cooking

Mister Rifleman

Survival with Style

Feasting Free on Wild Edibles

One Acre and Security

Wilderness Gear
You Can Make Yourself

BRADFORD ANGIER

Illustrations by ARTHUR J. ANDERSON

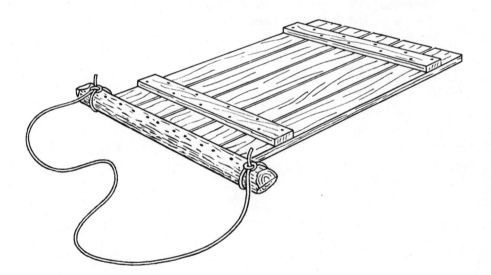

COLLIER BOOKS
A Division of Macmillan Publishing Co., Inc.
NEW YORK

Macmillan Publishing Co., Inc.
866 Third Avenue, New York, N.Y. 10022
Collier Macmillan Canada, Ltd.

Library of Congress Catalog Card Number: 72-93626

First Collier Books Edition 1973
Third Printing 1976
Printed in the United States of America

For Jim Rietmulder,
who made many things possible

Contents

Introduction

The pleasure of every outdoor trip is divided into three parts: the anticipation, the excitement of the adventure itself, and the memories. In many ways, the anticipation of a trip is the most pleasurable—the poring over maps, the shopping excursions, by catalog and in person, and even the drawing of plans on scraps of paper with a stubby pencil for that "necessary equipment" which will later prove either too costly for the budget or, perhaps, unobtainable.

This book is, in a way, for the outdoorsman or woman who is city-bound for eleven months of the year and who would like to enliven imprisonment in the concrete canyons by adding new items to the outdoor outfit. By doing so, he or she will be getting precisely what is needed at a price that most of us can afford and, at the same time, turning those soul-stirring dreams into year-round action.

Ernest Thompson Seton said, "Our purpose is to learn the outdoor life for its worth in the building up of our bodies; that we may go forth with the seeing eye and the thinking hand to learn the pleasant ways of the woods and of life." Among the gifts of God that separate man from the beasts is that of the *thinking hand*—hands so coordinated with the mind that man has been able to build from nature an almost completely new environment.

Craft with these hands, and its healing powers that stem, in part, from the going back to the simpler beginnings of things, is especially suited to the months of city imprisonment. The magic of handicraft can take you from the artificial and harried present to more basic, genuine realms of satisfying achievement, where nature softens even the most harsh traffic noises. In fact, you may find handicraft extending into your economic life even beyond the immediate saving of a few dollars. Newly discovered capacities for such skills have made more than one person rich.

At the very least, there are day-by-day lessons to be learned by the indoor making of some of the outdoor necessities. As local and world tensions mount, and as man, with his bounding knowledge, continues to produce potentially catastrophic weapons of destruction, there may come a time when it will be necessary for those few of us who survive to return to the cave, with its small, warm fire burning. In fact, an added bit of nature lore may mean survival itself.

When we go outdoors, it is to meet again, on intimate terms, the great natural world upon which our forefathers were so dependent and, even in these years of conquering atoms and space, upon which mankind is still dependent. No matter how hard we grope for what we call "civilization," without nature's basic resources man would quickly vanish from the earth.

Handicraft, then, is no simple subject or accomplishment. In making our own top-grade packsacks and sleeping bags, achievements which save us both money and stress, we are returning in some small and healthy way from the asphalt jungles to the simpler days when this continent was young and when Indians still happily used baskets to catch the sweet dripping sap of the maple.

WILDERNESS GEAR
YOU CAN MAKE YOURSELF

Carrying Gear

PACKBOARD

If you are a member of a backpacking family and need to fit packs to all growing members, making your own eminently comfortable and satisfactory packboards will really pay off.

Procure some strips of Sitka spruce, oak, or other strong wood, 2¼ inches wide by ½ inch thick. Cut two strips 28 inches long for the sides of the frame. Round the top ends but leave the bottom ends square.

Cut two other strips for the crosspieces, one 12 inches long and the other 15½ inches long. Join the two sidepieces with the two crosspieces, making a

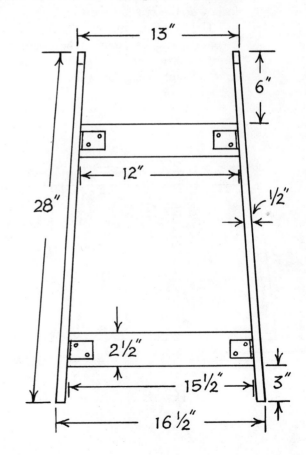

FIG-1

frame such as the one shown in Figure 1. The top of the upper cross member should come six inches down from the top ends of the sidepieces. The bottom of the lower cross member should be three inches above the bottom ends of the sidepieces.

The edge of the sidepieces and the flat of the crosspieces face the packer's back. Notice that the crosspieces are flush with the edge of the sidepieces farthest from the packer's back.

The crosspieces must be fastened to the sidepieces very accurately and strongly. Use angle irons with wood screws. Any machinist or blacksmith (if you happen to live where such an amateur or professional craftsman is handy) can turn out these right-angled pieces of metal in a very few minutes.

The resulting frame will be 13 inches wide at the top, 16½ inches wide at the bottom, 28 inches high, and 2½ inches thick. Using the same proportions, you can design as many different sizes as you need. Children, as well as adults, find these packs both rugged and comfortable. When the youngest member of the family finally outgrows his, so little money will be tied up in it that it may be cheerfully passed along to some young hiking friend without a qualm.

Over this frame, lace a cover of, say, twelve-ounce canvas, cut and made as shown in Figure 2. This is, in this instance, 28 inches wide at the top, 35 inches at the bottom, and 25 inches high. It covers the frame to within 1½ inches of the top and bottom.

Hem it all around and insert seven brass grommets along each side edge to accommodate the lacing. These grommets, along with inexpensive tools for inserting them, are obtainable from many sporting goods and hobby stores and from all tent and awning makers. On the side edge, hem the cover with two

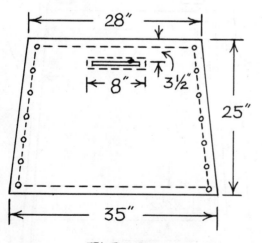

FIG-2

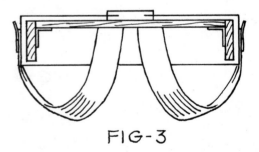

FIG-3

folds, fastening the grommets through both folds so they won't pull out.

Three and one-half inches down from the center of the top edge, there should be a horizontal slit, 8 inches long, strongly reinforced at the edges. This is for the shoulder straps to pass through.

This canvas cover is laced around the frame, drum tight, by means of strong cod line, smooth and heavy cotton line, passed through the grommets. The slit comes on the side toward the packer's back. The lacing is done on the side of the frame where the crosspieces are flush with the edges of the side-pieces, as per Figure 3. The edges with the grommets should not meet by about 2 inches, so that the canvas can be laced very tightly.

Incidentally, some packers do away with the canvas entirely, lacing such frames with long cord zigzagged back and forth through holes drilled about an inch apart along the sidepieces. This decreases the weight and increases the coolness, but the result is not as stable a canvas and will not hold up under heavier loads.

The upper ends of the shoulder straps are secured around the top cross-pieces of the frame at the center. They pass through the slit in the canvas, then around and over the bearer's shoulders, and are finally secured to the outside of the sidepieces of the frame six inches above the lower ends of these members, as shown in Figure 4. A piece of leather with a one-inch buckle is screwed to each of the sidepieces for this purpose.

The straps are best made of heavy chrome-tanned leather saturated with Neatsfoot oil. They should be 2 inches wide at the top and where they go over the shoulders, tapering to an inch at the bottom where they are secured to the buckles. Too wide a strap passing along the armpit causes chafing. Holes are

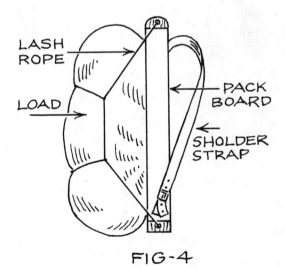

FIG-4

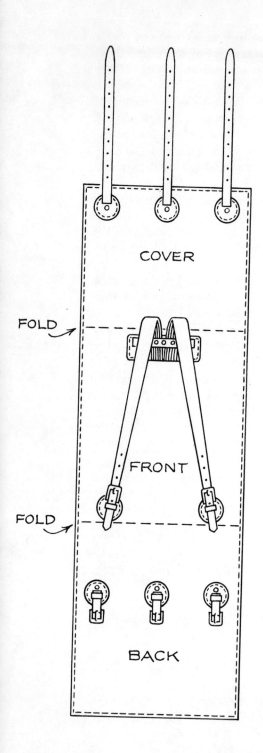

COVER

FOLD

FRONT

FOLD

BACK

punched in the straps to provide for adjustment in length. If you install these straps with the smooth side of the leather touching the shoulders, the pack will be easier to slip on and off.

These days, a firm, wide nylon webbing is available that can be tapered for the installation of buckles. Such webbing is nearly as good as leather for use as shoulder straps. Whether you use leather or fabric though, you will probably appreciate the use of shoulder pads, available so inexpensively that it's hardly worthwhile to bother sewing them at home. In a pinch, too, something such as heavy gloves shoved between straps and shoulders will make a considerable difference.

After the straps have been adjusted for length, they can be conveniently slipped over the shoulders, just as one puts on coat or suspenders. If you are alone, and no elevated surface such as a stump or log is nearby, merely stand the loaded pack upright on the ground. Sit and place your arms through the straps. Run your thumbs under these to make sure they lie flat on the shoulders. Then stand.

Figure 3 shows a section of this packboard as viewed looking down from the top. Figure 4 presents a side view, with the shoulder straps in position and with a load lashed onto the board. For this, holes are drilled in the top and bottom of the sidepieces of the frame through which to attach the lashing ropes.

PACKSACK

When you leave camp for a day of deer hunting, for instance, the chances are that you are carrying about ten cartridges in addition to those in your loaded rifle, a knife, watch, compass, waterproof match box, maybe a small tea pail, and lunch. A camera in its case may hang over your shoulder. At chest level, there probably are binoculars. Likely there will be other items bulging from your pockets: handkerchief, map, notebook, pencil, small first-aid kit, collapsible drinking cup, exposure meter, extra film, sunglasses, small mirror, piece of cord, and Carborundum stone.

A lot of hunters, if the weather is at all cold, start off in the chill of the morning with a down jacket. Many, in addition, so stuff their pockets and weigh down their belts that, particularly if they push through any tamarack with its shedding needles, they soon look and feel like an overloaded Christmas tree. The chances are that by now they would like to shed that jacket, but they have nowhere to carry it.

All or most of this impedimenta is often desirable on a day's hunt. That particular system of carrying it, however, is unnecessarily handicapping. What is needed is a light packsack. After you have carried one for three or four days, you will never notice you have it with you. All discomfort is gone. Nothing dangles or catches. Your belt does not cut into you the way it did before. Your pockets do not bulge or press.

It is often hard to find just the right packsack for this sort of thing, but you can make one yourself with very little trouble. It will be good for a lifetime.

The illustrations speak for themselves, as there is nothing at all complicated about the job. Twelve-ounce canvas works fine. You'll end up with a pack of about twenty-eight inches square, with an adjustable flap held down by three straps and buckles—a pack that will ride comfortably close to your back, well out of the way, even if the going becomes tight.

Although you can use fabric, the carrying straps will be most comfortable over the years if they are made of heavy leather, softened with Neatsfoot oil, two inches wide where they go over the shoulders and tapering to one inch wide where they are secured to buckles. Holes are punched in these straps to provide for their adjustment in length.

Be sure that these shoulder straps are long enough so that the pack can sag down into the hollow of the back with more than half its weight resting on the hips. Thus, its burden will not be felt on the shoulders, and your center of gravity will remain low enough to assure better and safer balance.

POUCH

Packing for outdoor trips will be easier, and in camp it'll later be easier to locate what you want, if you'll relegate each group of items—handkerchiefs, underwear, and socks, for instance—to its own small, separate ditty bag. Handy for these are drawstring pouches, such as those you can lastingly and attractively put together with soft leather.

To make the illustrated pouch, complete with a corner hole from which it can be conveniently hung beside your sleeping bag, draw on transparent paper a pattern of the desired size, perhaps with a 1½-foot diameter. You can use a pencil attached to a held string to give you your circle. Spread this pattern over the drawing in the book, center to center, and project the holes out to your pattern's edge by tracing a line from the common center through each hole in the printed sketch. You now have functional spacing for the holes on your transparent pattern.

Then cut out the leather for the pouch and for the two small attachments. Sew on these attachments. Slits will do for the holes. Or, for a more finished job, use a punch, eyelets, and an eyelet-setting tool. Or you can get a special attachment for your plier-action punch to perform this task.

Finally, cut two leather laces or use two lengths of heavy cord. Starting through one pair of the holes and finishing in the opposite pair, the thongs should lace all the way around the pouch in opposite directions. Conclude by knotting the end of each thong to keep the pouch from opening too wide. You'll end up with a handy container that should give you good service for a lifetime.

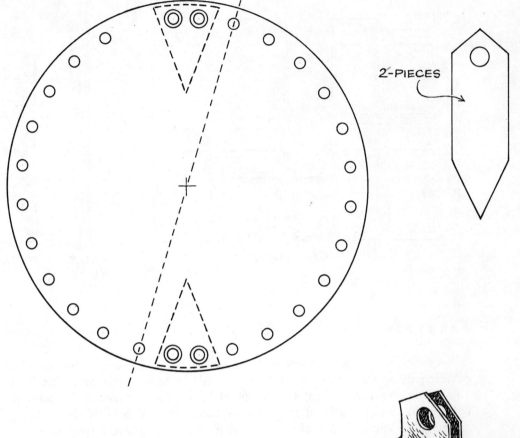

2-PIECES

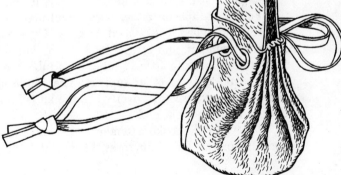

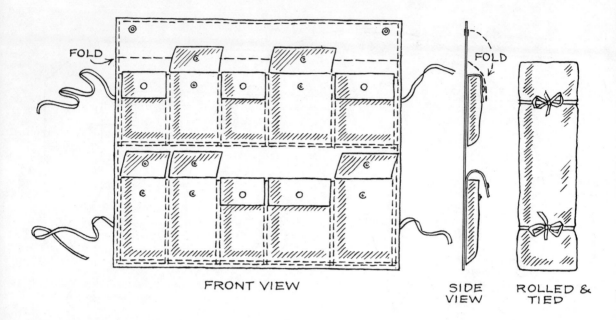

FRONT VIEW   SIDE   ROLLED &
                             VIEW   TIED

CARRYALL

A fabric roll of pockets always comes in handy, and I keep one suspended conveniently on the wall of our log cabin, ready to take on camping trips. Such a holder is easily made from a rectangle of heavy duck, unbleached muslin, or lightweight canvas, outfitted with two or three rows of pockets that may be graduated in size and each of which may, if you choose, have a snap flap.

Foot-long tapes at either corner will make such a contraption easy to hold in a roll and, when it is opened, to hang. Or, along the top edge of the carryall, make buttonholes, and on the back of the kit, sew buttons so that the top can be buttoned back to form a tube. This tube can then be buttoned over a tent rope, a tree limb, or other support once you're in the wilderness. Leave a flap at the bottom to use as a cover when the kit is folded, and then sew on a tie tape only at either bottom end.

You can even make a smaller "kitchen" edition, with a single row of three pockets, for carrying your forks, knives, and spoons.

PANNIERS

Throughout the mountains and foothills of western North America, from the dusty mesquite of Mexico to the luring Arctic Circle, almost all the unspoiled wilderness remaining is at least two or three days' travel from the railroad or nearest road. Outdoorsmen have to pack their outfits and supplies into these regions and, although these days aircraft are taking over to a certain extent, the most common method of transport is still with pack animals. When you're journeying with horses or mules, you'll need panniers.

There is no standard size for such panniers. Most of them, the better ones, measure (on the outside) about twenty-two inches long, fifteen inches high, and nine inches wide from front to back. Packers in wooded country prefer the bottoms angled back so that the two panniers, one on each side, will not stick out too far from the animal and catch trees. Such a base six inches wide is functional.

The top, bottom, and sides can be made of ⅜- or ½-inch waterproof plywood and the ends of ⅞-inch pine or spruce. To prevent mice and chipmunks from getting at the contents, food panniers can be lined with metal or with rustproof screening. Notches on the front edges, shown in the drawing, are made for lash ropes that secure the pannier on the sawbuck saddle. Hinges and fasteners can be either metal or leather.

Various camp outfitters sell panniers, or kyacks as they are also called, made of fiberboard and plywood. But you can also build them yourself, as most bushmen still do. Some are fashioned along similar lines of the heaviest canvas. Especially picturesque, although not as practical as the described wooden variety, are those made of tough, untanned cowhide, laced together with the hair outside.

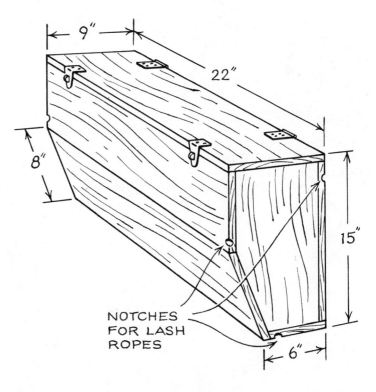

NOTCHES FOR LASH ROPES

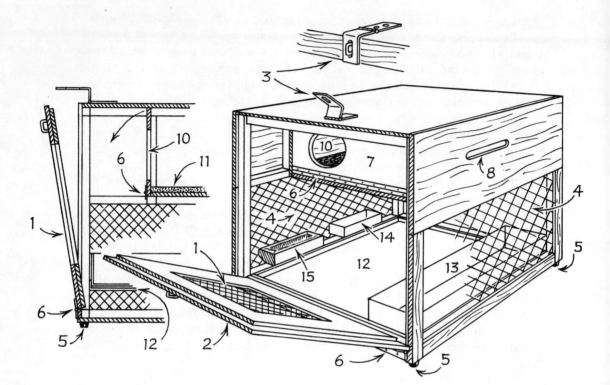

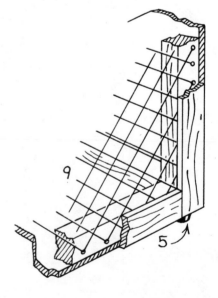

ANIMAL CRATE

You often want to take your small or medium-sized pet on one of your outdoor trips and, occasionally, crating is necessary to get it safely and happily to the jumping-off place. Lt. Col. Lyman P. Davison, who has a magnificent domesticated wolf, Shane, as a car and house companion, devised the following very practical plywood box with this in mind. It can be efficiently used the year round as a permanent shelter as well.

1. Access door showing arrangement of screen.
2. Front door, open, showing construction.
3. Hasp, open and closed position, showing design.
4. Side screens.
5. Furniture castors or rubber mounts may be used to keep crate off ground.
6. Piano hinges.
7. Upper chamber door.
8. Slots, one each side, for easy carrying of crate.
9. Construction details.
10. Access port, upper chamber.
11. Air-foam pad covering floor of upper chamber.
12. Removable floor tray, constructed of aluminum or galvanized sheet metal.
13. Removable litter box.
14. Removable food tray.
15. Removable and unspillable water dish.

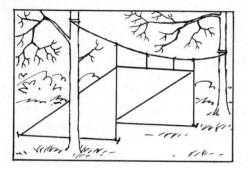

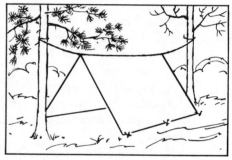

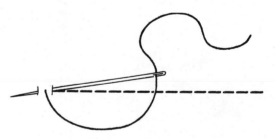

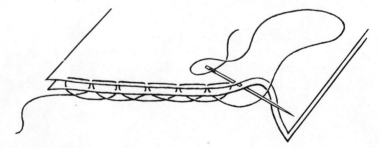

BACK STITCH

2

Shelter

TARPAULIN

When I'm camping with a pack train, I carry a light, 7½-by-12-foot tarpaulin, rolled behind my saddle. Such a versatile tarp also goes with me while I'm canoeing.

The tarp I've long used I made myself by overlapping and sewing together three 12-foot strips of water-repellent, green fabric 32 inches wide, then adding an inch hem all around. The corners, I reinforced by stitching on 4-inch-square pieces of the same material. Half-inch grommets at each corner, midway along each side, and halfway between each of those holes on the two longer sides, completed the job. Through each of the grommets, I subsequently added a 6-foot quarter-inch rope.

Ordinarily I pitch this tarp at a single 45° slant, with the two sides bushed in and a cheerful fire burning companionably in front. It can also be erected several other ways, depending on the circumstances, as suggested by the illustrations.

Your choice of tarpaulin material will be a matter of compromise, for the heavier the fabric, the greater both the abrasion resistance and the tear strength. Yet you'll likely want the finished product to be as lightweight as reasonable.

Nylon is a possibility, but its slipperiness makes it an often sleazy fabric, prone to fray badly unless finished seams are used or the edges melted to fuse the yarns together. Too, the very elasticity of nylon thread, which makes it excellent for adjustment to stress, causes it to be difficult to use in home sewing machines. Even though you can get around this with practice and with proper tension adjustment, the old dependable cotton still has vital advantages, not the least of which is its ability to accept and retain water-repellent treatments.

The best tentage fabric at the time of this writing is a cotton reinforced with nylon or Dacron. Even with this material, though, a water-repellent treatment must be periodically repeated. The direst enemy of water repellents is dirt, by the way, so keep your equipment clean.

Nylon has ample strength even in ultra-light weaves, although there will be trouble in waterproofing it. A good combination for lightweight waterproof tentage then, is a layer of two-ounce cotton for the covering proper and a top

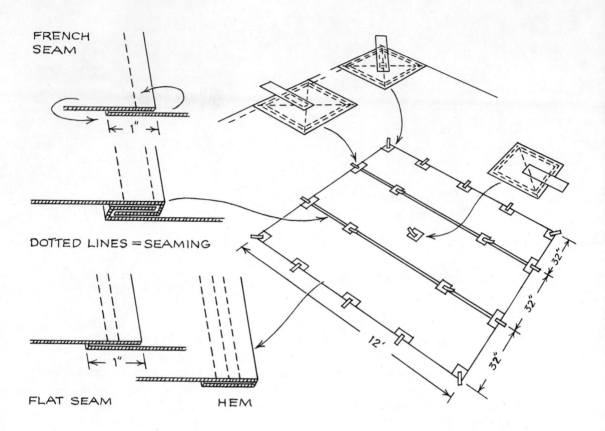

FRENCH
SEAM

DOTTED LINES = SEAMING

FLAT SEAM   HEM

layer of one-ounce plastic-coated nylon for a rain fly. The soundest idea, in any event, is to procure your material from a reliable tent company (many will mail free catalogs).

Because of the amount of stitching involved, a sewing machine—which can usually be rented if one is not already in your home—is almost essential in the making of tentage, sleeping bags, and clothing. The lock-stitch foot is preferable to the chain-stitch foot, as the seams of the former will not pull out. Rotary bobbins will sew more rapidly than the long-shuttle varieties. For those hard-to-reach spots that have to be sewn by hand, a pair of sturdy needles and a thimble will do the job, plus a little beeswax to strengthen the thread and, if it is nylon, to keep it from kinking.

A sturdy stitch for hand sewing is illustrated. Such a backstitch assures a dependable, strong, continuous seam.

So you sew your pieces of material together to make a tarp of the desired dimensions, hemming the two cut edges or, if the material is nylon, fusing them with a hot iron. Where the grommets—or, if you prefer, tie tapes—are to be affixed, sew on reinforcements cut from the fabric itself. Four-inch-square corner reinforcements will be fine, while oblongs, 2-by-4-inches, will suffice along the edges. Conclude the operation by adding half-inch grommets, or, if you're using them, tie tapes, each a two-foot length of twill tape that is folded in the middle where it is attached to the tarp.

If you wish to dye or decorate the tarpaulin, now is the time to do it. Then, unless you have used an already waterrepellent material, end the project by waterproofing the covering. Begin by pitching this tight and taut some sunny morning. Take a pound of paraffin, inexpensively procurable in cakes at most grocery stores. Cut it into shavings and dissolve these in one gallon of turpentine. The process can be hastened by placing the can in a receptacle of hot water. Keep it away from flames, however, as it is quite flammable. Then paint the fabric liberally with the solution, preferably while both are warm, and let the tarp stand until thoroughly dry.

WHELEN LEAN-TO TENT

"Most men are needlessly poor all of their lives because they think they must have such a house as their neighbors have," an old woodsman by the name of Henry David Thoreau observed more than a century ago. "Consider how slight a shelter is absolutely necessary."

The Whelen Lean-To Tent, designed by the old friend who wrote *On Your Own in the Wilderness* with me, remains my favorite. Col. Townsend Whelen's pattern, which is shown, will accommodate one or two campers, sleeping with their sides to the front. The previous discussion of materials and sewing methods, considered in connection with tarpaulins, holds here. Allow one inch around the edges for hemming. The other key details follow:

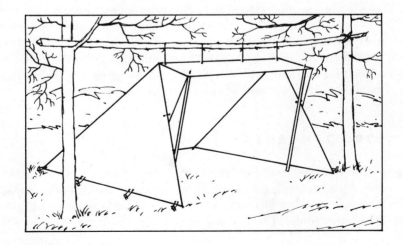

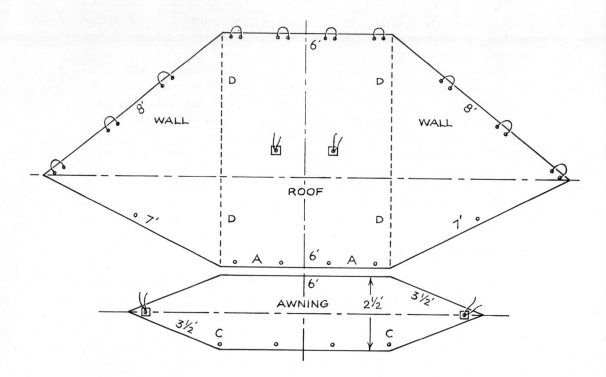

A A—Tape ridge with outside loops for ridge pole, and two loops on under side for clothing pole.

B B—Loops or cords sewed to outside of roof in which to insert poles when necessary to take the leak-prone belly from roof in snow or heavy rain.

C C—Large grommets, one-inch diameter, in which to insert sharpened poles which keep awning extended to the front when desired.

D D—Loops sewed inside at junction of roof and walls from which to hang mosquito bar when needed.

Again, you should pitch this tent with its back to the prevailing wind. Then a brisk fire in front, with a wall of rocks or green logs behind as a reflector in the coldest weather, will afford light and perfect comfort.

FORESTER TENT

If you need to cut weight or cost, the Forester Tent is a good solution. It is one of the best tents ever devised for a chronic woods-loafer, particularly for one who yearns to live close to nature and who objects to spending any of his outdoor hours confined in a closed canvas cell.

The Forester Tent is the cheapest of all wilderness tents to make yourself or to buy. It is the easiest and quickest to pitch. Considering its weight and bulk, it is the most comfortable in which to live and do your few camp chores. With the exception of the Whelen Lean-To Tent, it is the easiest to warm with a campfire in front.

The one weak point of the Forester, at first glance anyway, is that if you try to flyproof it, you ruin its inexpensiveness and its functional simplicity. In bug time, however, it is an easy matter to buy a mosquito bar for a dollar or two, or to make one yourself, as detailed elsewhere in this book, and to hang or stake a net closure over your bed.

The Forester Tent is triangular in shape. The smallest practical dimensions for one man, or for two who do not mind a bit of crowding, is about seven feet wide at the open front, three feet wide at the back, and seven feet deep from front to rear. The peak of such a model should stand about six feet above the ground in front, while the triangular rear will be some three feet high. With the entire tent open to the fire in front, the angles are such that heat and light will be reflected throughout the sheltered area. It is, of course, a tent for real wilderness where poles and firewood are plentiful.

The tent is usually pitched with three poles and eight sticks cut at the campsite. The ridgepole should be long enough to extend from the peak and to pass down and out through the hole at the top of the back wall, at such a tilt that it will rest on the ground about three feet behind the tent. Two shorter poles are arranged in front as shares and, holding the ridgepole at their crossing, run from the peak to the front corners.

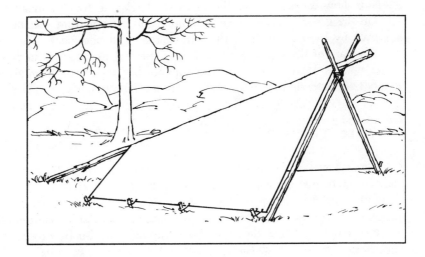

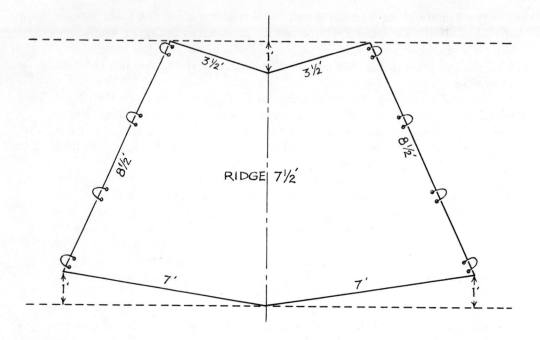

The pattern illustrated is for one or two campers, with beds arranged along the side walls. The model we use is made of closely woven, waterproofed cotton weighing five ounces per square yard, cut and sewn to the shape and dimensions shown, with one inch being allowed around the edges for hemming.

Note how the bottom of the sides set back one foot to make the tent sit right on the ground. To manage this, cut your pattern from rectangular canvas as shown by the dotted lines, then angle the front and back. The rear wall is cut off square at the top, and when this is stitched to the main body of the tent at the rear, it leaves a hole at the top of the back wall through which the ridgepole is extended. Total weight is about four pounds.

PLASTIC TUBING

Here's a way to have a tent, for a few pennies, that's light to carry and a cinch to pitch. Just get a piece of plastic tubing about eight feet long, available at many outfitters. Put up by running a rope through it to serve as a ridge and tying this several feet high between two trees. No pegs are necessary; the weight of the occupant anchors the tube. Such tubing can also be obtained in longer lengths, say fifteen feet, so that one camper can sleep at each open end.

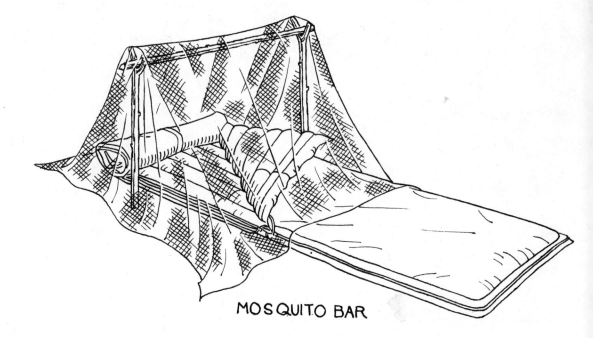

MOSQUITO BAR

MOSQUITO BAR

An effective mosquito and fly defense for tentless sleeping can be fashioned from a few yards of preferably black or other dark mosquito netting, such as fine-net bobbinet or even cheesecloth. Dark, rather than light, netting is suggested for two reasons. It's easier to see out through and the darker colors attract fewer insects than, for example, white.

Use the finest net you can find and sew it into a sort of pup-tent shape, long enough to drape loosely over the bed once it is in its place. Or, if you want, make it just large enough to drape over your head. Hang this canopy over your sleeping bag, using something such as a tripod, two light sticks, or perhaps string suspended from overhead branches.

Just be sure there is ample netting to cover your hands and shoulders so that you won't rest against it during the night. If you do, every bloodthirsty bug in the woods will seem to find that spot, and you'll be miserable. To be doubly safe, in fact, use insect dope on your hands at least. If you have an insect spray, apply that to the canopy to keep the hum of the winged pests away, and to exterminate that one mosquito that always seems to get inside the net.

Incidentally, if you're sleeping in the car and desire ventilation without bugs, get some 3-by-3-foot squares of fine screening material, again preferably some such color as black or dark green for better outward vision. Drape the netting over the outside of the open car door. Fold the top of the netting over the top of the door so that it will be held fast when the door is shut. Tape the bottom of the material to the door below the window.

To protect your face and neck while hiking in a particularly insect-ridden area, sew netting to brim of your hat and drape to shoulders.

Fire Making and Lighting the Dark

3

FUZZSTICKS

Fire is often your most basic need in the wilderness. With it you can warm yourself, dry clothing which, in a cold climate, can mean the difference between life and death, enjoy a comfortable night, cook your meals, and even signal for help.

Wood is the most common fuel by far in the silent places, and, if you are starting your fire with it under adverse conditions, it will pay you to make fuzzsticks, firesticks, feathersticks, or whatever you want to call them.

These are surer and more effective for fire starting than just bare kindling, and with practice you'll be able to manufacture three or four of them in half as many minutes. In the far north, I use three every morning to start the fire in our log cabin stove, and it is a mark of courtesy in these regions to leave kindling, firewood, and a few fuzzsticks whenever you quit an abode.

The fuzzstick is made by shaving a stick of dry kindling again and again, leaving the ribbons of wood attached so that they curl away from the parent stick in a sort of fan. You'll need at least three of these, and, when conditions are drastic, I commonly add another one to start the blaze quickly and without fail.

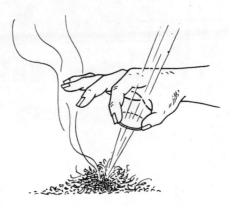

MAGNIFIER

Have you ever lit a fire with water? If the water is frozen, find a clear piece of ice. Experiment with shaving this with your knife, then finally smoothing it in the warm hands, until you have a lens capable of pinpointing the sun.

If the weather is warm, you're still not beaten. Hold the curved crystals of two watches of similar size, or even compass crystals, back to back. It does not matter if these are made of unbreakable plastic instead of glass as long as they are clear. Fill the space between the crystals with clear water. Then hold this contrived enlarging-lens so as to converge the sun's rays in a point hot enough to start tinder glowing. Blow the glowing tinder into fire, then thrust it among the campfire makings.

FLINT AND STEEL

The flint and steel of the "buckskin years" work as well today. The spark may be made these days by striking the back of your knife against a piece of flint (perhaps one you've set with plastic into the bottom of a match case). If there is no recognizable flint in your vicinity, experiment with other hard stones. Quartzite, jasper, nephrite, obsidian, jadeite, iron pyrite, and agate are among the rocks that will also work.

You don't even need a knife. The back of a hatchet will work readily. So will any steel. Iron will also do.

Holding your hands closely over your dry tinder, strike the stone flatly with your knife blade or other small piece of metal with a sharp, downward, scraping motion that will send sparks skittering into the midst of the fire-makings.

Incidentally, the Eskimo in northern Canada often carried two fist-sized chunks of fool's gold. Iron pyrite is easily recognizable because it ordinarily seems to be brightened with more flecks of gold than many a piece of gold-bearing quartz. To get a spark, just strike the two rocks together. If no fool's gold is at hand, try to locate two other stones that will spark when rubbed briskly against each other. Many have this property.

Why not make a leather pouch to hold the necessary items for starting some of your campfires as our ancestors did? All you need is a couple of pieces of soft leather about 8 inches square. The finished pouch can be either square or half-round. It should measure at least 6-by-8 inches to hold the items needed for flint-and-steel fire lighting.

To make a square pouch, cut one piece of leather about 2 inches larger all around than the other. If your pouch is to be half-round, make one piece of a half-pie shape and the other round, about 2 inches larger than the half-pie bit. Punch holes ½ inch back from the edges of the smaller piece and ½ inch apart around all sides but the top. Place this segment evenly on the large piece and make companion holes in the larger leather. Now, with a thin thong, lace the two pieces neatly together, finally tying the ends with a square knot at the back of the pouch.

Fringe the extra part of the larger piece up to the top corners. Then trim the surplus to form a flap that will fold down over the pouch. This flap can be fastened with a button, preferably one of those described elsewhere in this book, that is attached to a leather thong. For instance, a bit of antler or bone may be used. A slit in the flap provides the buttonhole.

For the kit itself, you'll need a piece of hard steel such as a short length of broken file, a piece of flint, and some charred wicking. Any lamp or candle wicking will do if you first burn one edge of it. Charred cotton cloth works, too. You'll also need some shredded cedar bark or other tinder—clothing lint, absorbent cotton, the dry, pulverized fluff from pussy willows, down from bird nests, pulverized birch bark, etc.

To make the fire, place the charred fabric atop the flint, the blackened edges close to the edge of the stone. With the steel, strike a hard, glancing blow down and across the edge of the flint, making sparks. These will be caught in the charred fabric where they will spread into a glowing line. Place a ball of your tinder around this and blow through it. When the tinder ignites, nest it at the bottom of some prepared light kindling, and soon everything will be blazing.

BOW AND DRILL

Fire can also be started by friction as with the bow and drill technique, the fire saw, the fire thong, etc. When I was a Boy Scout in New England, we used to practice with the first of these for our own entertainment and edification. It's not a bad way to pass a rainy afternoon in front of the fireplace, and in a pinch it could one day save your life.

Briefly, make a strong bow, strung loosely with a shoelace, thong, or string. Use this to spin a soft, dry shaft in an easily handled block of hardwood. This will produce a powdery black dust which eventually will catch a spark. When smoke begins to rise, you should have enough spark to light your fire. Then lift the block, add tinder, and begin blowing on it.

In North America, both the drill and the fire board are often made of one of the following woods: fir, balsam, cottonwood, white or red cedar, linden, tamarack, cypress, basswood, yucca, poplar, or willow.

The drill can be a straight, well-seasoned stick from about ¼ to ¾ of an inch thick and approximately 12 to 15 inches long. The top end of the drill

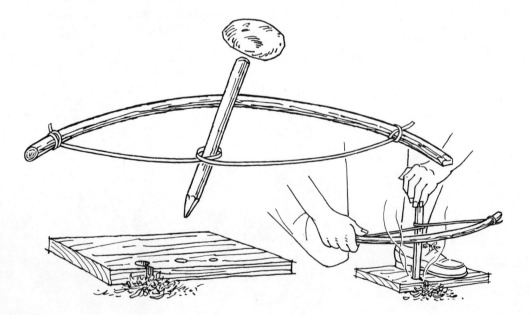

should be as smoothly rounded as possible so that it will turn easily in the socket. However, a maximum of friction is desirable on the other end which, consequently, must be blunter.

The sole function of the socket is to hold the top of the turning drill. Inasmuch as it is grasped with one hand, it may be an easily held knot of wood with a hollow formed in its underneath. It may also be, of course, a block made for that very purpose. Or, if you are near water, it is frequently possible to find a slick stone with a smooth depression eroded in one side. The socket may be oiled or waxed with native materials such as animal fat or bayberries, etc., so as to permit the drill to rotate more freely.

The bow is occasionally made from a limber stick which, if strung more tightly, might be used to shoot darts or arrows. More often, though, you see a substantial branch with a natural crook already in it. The bow string, which may be anything from a leather shoelace to tightly braided strips of clothing, is tied at both ends with enough slack remaining to permit it to be wound once about the drill.

The dimensions of the fire board, which can be split out of a dry log and then split again, may be whatever you can handle easily. The board or slab, in other words, can be an inch thick and four or five inches wide. You'll want it to be long enough to be held under one of your feet.

Using a knife or even a sharp stone, begin a hole about ¾ of an inch in from the edge of the fire board. Round out this hole, at the same time fitting it to the end of the drill, by turning the drill with the bow. Finally, cut a notch through to this cup from the edge of the board. The sides of this slot generally slant so that it is noticeably wider at the bottom, permitting the hot black powder that is produced by the drilling to fall as readily as possible into the tinder that is laid at the base of the notch.

When you're ready, the tinder is massed beneath the slot in the fire board. If you are right-handed, kneel on your right knee and put your left foot as securely as possible on one end of the fire board. Take the bow in your right hand. Loop the string once around the drill. Place the drill in the hole made in the fire board.

Pressing on the drill, spin it by drawing the bow back and forth in smooth sweeps, making these as long as the string will conveniently permit. At this stage, you might try dropping a few grains of sand into the hole to build up the friction. In any event, the hole will eventually begin to smoke. Spin the bow even more rapidly now. Press down more determinedly on the drill.

Hot black powder will start to spill into the tinder. Continue drilling, for the stronger a spark you can start reddening there, the quicker you'll be able to breathe it into fire. Everything finally will seem ready. Then carefully remove the drill. Blow gently into the slot until you can see a glow.

Then lift both tinder and fire board if that is easiest. Press the tinder easily about the gleam. When the spark finally starts spreading, lift the board out of the way so you can fan and blow on the heat more freely. Gently continue feeding air to the area until the tinder bursts into flame.

FIRE SAW

The fire saw consists of two pieces of wood that are sawed vigorously against each other to make a spark, a method of firemaking commonly used in the jungle. Split bamboo or some other soft wood can be utilized as the rubbing stick and the dry sheath of the coconut flower as the wood base. The illustration explains the process.

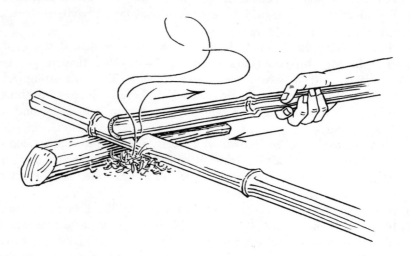

FIRE THONG

The thong can be a strip of dry rattan, preferably about ¼ inch in diameter and 2 feet in length. You'll also need a dry stick.

Prop this stick off the ground on a log or rock. Split the elevated end of the stick. Hold open with a wedge. Place a small wad of tinder in the split, leaving enough room behind it to insert the thong. Then, securing the stick with your foot or knee, work the thong rapidly back and forth until the tinder starts to glow, whereupon it will be possible to blow it into flame.

WATERPROOF MATCHES

Another worthwhile project is to ready waterproof matches for that emergency supply every camper should always have in his outfit. One easy way to go about this is to get some empty 12- and 16-gauge shotgun shells, perhaps from a nearby skeet field or trapshooting range, and dip them into melted paraffin. Fill the smaller shell with long, wooden, "strike-anywhere" kitchen matches. Slip the 12-gauge shell over this to make a telescoped container. Now

dip the closed package in the melted paraffin, and you'll have some really waterproof matches.

Some outdoorsmen fill the end of the inside shell with small bits of cotton, which can be used for tinder, to keep the matches from rattling, then seal the joining with tape before dipping the whole contrivance into wax a second time. For added utility file some notches into the brass end of one of the shells to serve as a striking surface when everything else is wet and smooth.

Incidentally, a waterproof matchcase that will float if dropped overboard can be fashioned from about four inches of light aluminum tubing. Jam a cork into one end, then cut it off flush with the end of the tube. Fill the tube with wooden kitchen matches. Fit another cork over the remaining open end, but do not cut this one off. Dip the whole thing in melted paraffin, and you'll be ready for that boat or canoe trip into the wilderness.

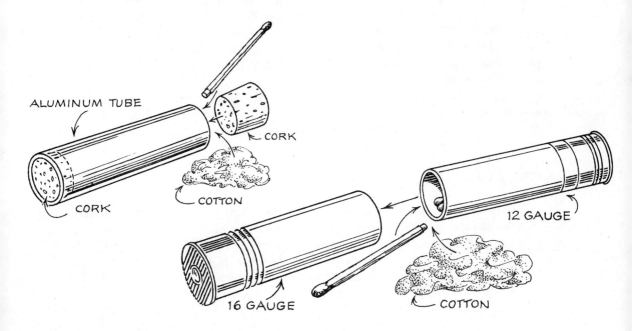

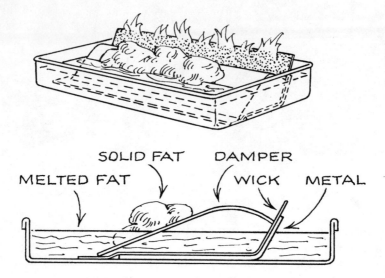

SOLID FAT   DAMPER

MELTED FAT   WICK   METAL

ESKIMO KOODLIK

Any flat can or liquid-holding stone or metal container will serve as a functional and picturesque koodlik, the Eskimo's fat-lamp. When you do have fat to burn, the only other necessity is a piece of cloth, absorbent cotton, or moss for a wick, plus a sloping surface to support this.

Lubricating oil can be similarly burned in a koodlik, but the wick will have to be trimmed more precisely to keep the flame below the smoking point. Then as the level of the oil diminishes, the flame may follow it down the wick to cause additional smoking. A primitive damper, easily fashioned out of a bent piece of sheet metal from a can or made of foil, will help prevent this, allowing closer control of the light.

Naturally, gasoline, which is extremely explosive, cannot be used in a koodlik except under extreme wilderness conditions. Then perhaps two or three drops can be used to ease the lighting of the wick.

CANDLES

If, when it's stormy and windy, you use your first match to light a candle, then let the stronger flame from that kindle your campfire. You will always be able to count upon starting your outdoor fire surely and swiftly—an achievement that, in an emergency, may save someone's life. Candles, too, are an easy and inexpensive way of providing light for camp and, especially, a tent. The sort of stout, rugged tapers most satisfactory for outdoor uses are often best made at home, and you'll likely find that creating your own candles can be more than an interesting, money-saving hobby. It's also an adventure, partly because the origins of this sort of light go back further toward caveman eons than we can trace.

You can use the fragrant beeswax for your candles if a source of supply is available to you, as per my *One Acre and Security*. You can even provide yourself with candles for free by utilizing wild bayberries (*Myrica*) as I suggest in *More Free-for-the-Eating Wild Foods*. Lacking either of these, buy some household paraffin wax at your store, such as the clean-burning and nonsmoking Gulfwax, inexpensively available in ½-pound bars that are sold separately or four to a 1-pound box. This wax, I find, has a melting point that contributes to its ready release from most candle molds.

Excellent wicks can be bought at most hardware stores—just ask for car-

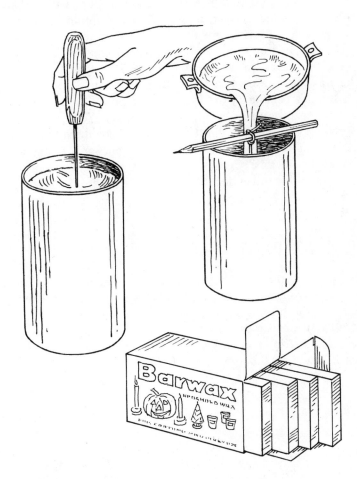

penter's or bricklayer's chalk line. Or, make your own wicking by soaking cotton string for a few hours in a solution of one tablespoon of salt and two table- spoons of borax in a cup of water. Dip the dried wick in melted wax to stiffen it, then twist.

You can make some handy little candles from empty paper shotgun shells, too. Insert a wick in the center of each empty shell and pour in melted paraffin. These little candles will burn ardently, won't tip over easily, will not bend with hot weather, are easy to carry, and are fine for wet-weather fire-starting.

In a pinch, waxed milk containers make emergency candles. Set one on a metal plate or heap of sand and put dirt or pebbles in the bottom to keep it from blowing over. Then light the top. The container will burn for about ten minutes and give off a pretty fair light even in a drizzle or rain.

Molds are everywhere, though—for example, the tubes on which waxed paper is rolled. Or, make your own with fine, moist sand. Always melt the wax in a double boiler over low heat, slowly and gradually. If the wax should flame, immediately place a lid over it or extinguish the fire with baking soda. Never use water and, for that matter, never splash water into hot wax.

You can get your wick into the candle by several methods. If practical, tie the wick to a pencil or similar crosspiece and suspend it in the empty mold, a small weight attached to the bottom of the wick to hold it vertical while you pour the wax into the container. Another way is to insert an ice pick into the candle while it's cooling in the mold. If the hole fills before you can shove in the wick, reinsert the probe as often as necessary. You can also use a warm ice pick to make a hole in a candle that's already cooled. No matter how you insert the wick, pour a bit of melted wax after it to anchor it in the taper.

Functional, all this? Consider that more candles are burned today, nearly a century after the invention of the electric light, than when Thomas Alva Edison first flicked his fateful switch.

CANDLE HOLDERS

Candles have the fluttering delicacy of the waning campfire. Camp holders for them vary from horizontal tin cans which protect the flame from the wind (the short candle being shoved upward through a hole punched in the side) to innumerable rustic variations. One of the simpler variations is a cleft, green stick securing a strip of birch bark which, in turn, grasps the base of the taper. Another is made in the rounded top of a slab in which holes are bored or whittled.

TORCH

The temptation to remain in good fishing and hunting country after dusk is sometimes irresistible, and you may not have a flashlight to show you the way

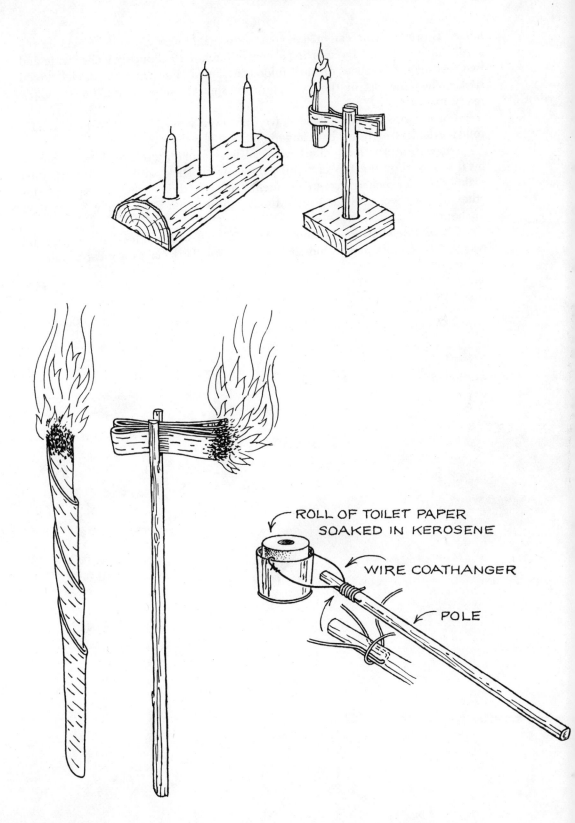

ROLL OF TOILET PAPER
SOAKED IN KEROSENE

WIRE COATHANGER

POLE

home. However, you can make yourself a wilderness torch that will last a surprisingly long time by inserting sheets of birch bark about six inches wide and two feet long, or a sheet of bark folded in similar dimensions, in a cleft green stick. When the last of the bark starts to sputter, have an additional supply ready to insert.

For a carried torch that will give light even longer, bind two long, tightly rolled cylinders of birch bark together and light the top.

Or, with a little more effort, you can have a pitch torch ready for nightfall by first pounding the top of a substantial green stick until it is fibrous, then soaking this in melted evergreen pitch. Once the first layer congeals, plaster others thickly over it. Such a pitch torch will give you a cheerfully bright light for hours.

Closer to civilization, attach a can to a pole with clothes-hanger wire, fill with a roll of toilet paper, and soak in kerosene. This makes a great torch.

Keeping Warm at Night

4

SLEEPING BAG

A top-grade sleeping bag is often the most expensive item of outdoor equipment you'll buy, but in this instance, too, you can make your own. Temperatures around our home in Hudson Hope, British Columbia, sometimes fall more than 60° below zero, and the bag described will keep you warm outdoors in such cold, while still being comfortable during the mountain summers. Claire Barkley, sourdough friend and neighbor, made such a sleeping robe for her husband, Joe, who has spent many a winter freighting for the Indian department across the frozen muskegs of the North to the Graham River, riding alone in an open sleigh. The resulting 72-by-84-inch bag is the best one I've ever seen for the purpose, and here is how Claire inexpensively made it.

You'll need 5 yards of 36-inch wide grey kersey, 7½ yards of 28-inch wide brown nylon, 13½ yards of feather ticking, 36 inches wide, and a dozen lift-the-dot fasteners, plus the filler. If you want to save money, chicken feathers will do for the filler, or you can purchase the best-of-all, white waterfowl down, from a sleeping-bag manufacturer. Handiest is down already enclosed in tubes, available from such a distributor as Trailwise, 1615 University Avenue, Berkeley, California 94703 (which, incidentally, also handles the other necessary items). With already distributed down, you will not need the ticking.

If you want, you can substitute a lightweight, water-repellent duck for the exterior. Cotton flannel will save you money as the liner. Zippers are, of course, available, although I've yet to own a zippered sleeping bag that did not finally break down under rugged daily usage.

Cut your 5-yard strip of kersey in half to make a pair of 2½-yard-wide strips. Join these lengthwise. Measure 3 strips 3½ inches by 80 inches, sewing these between the kersey and the nylon, raw edges together. Sew across the foot of the bag. Now turn right side out. There will then be a strip of nylon showing on each side of the kersey on the inside of the bag lengthwise.

This is the time to insert the feather ticking into the kersey and nylon envelope. Catch-stitch the bottom of the filler to the raw edges of the envelope at the bottom to hold everything in place. Do the same thing along the sides.

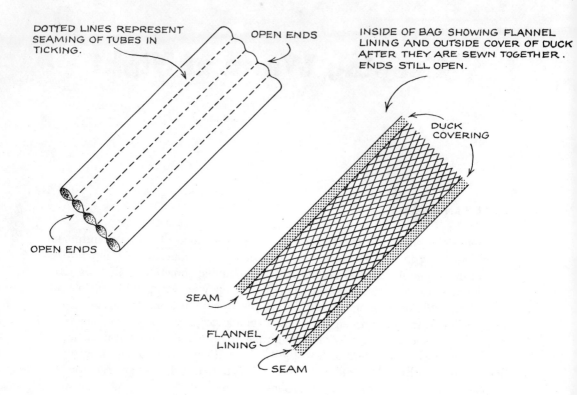

DOTTED LINES REPRESENT SEAMING OF TUBES IN TICKING.

OPEN ENDS

INSIDE OF BAG SHOWING FLANNEL LINING AND OUTSIDE COVER OF DUCK AFTER THEY ARE SEWN TOGETHER. ENDS STILL OPEN.

DUCK COVERING

OPEN ENDS

SEAM

FLANNEL LINING

SEAM

Next, sew the neck line of the nylon and kersey together, turning the nylon's raw seams in ⅜ inch, catching the ticking now and then. Hem the extra length of kersey at the top.

Fold the sleeping bag inside out. At the center fold at the bottom, sew a triangle, 2 inches by 1½ inches, across the corner to form a boxlike corner and to bring the foot of the bag to the 36-inch flange of the material.

If snaps are used, put them on half of the bottom of the bag where the strip was sewn between nylon and kersey, placing the corresponding part of the snap on the outside of the flange of the nylon near the bag's bottom. Continue up the side, after you've sewn several seams lengthwise on the edge that has no flange for snaps. Stitch the two layers of material together, making a band about 1¼ inches wide upon which to set the other half of the fasteners. This is not necessary when you're using a zipper.

The snaps are to be on the outside of the bag and on the under side of the flange. Then when the bag is closed and in use, there will be protection from drafts by a roll of material along its edges.

All this proceeds logically, step by step, and is much simpler to do than to describe. Such a sleeping bag will be good for a lifetime of hard usage. When

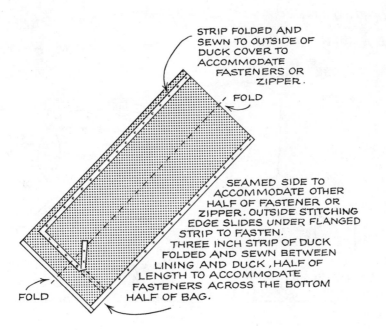

STRIP FOLDED AND
SEWN TO OUTSIDE OF
DUCK COVER TO
ACCOMMODATE
FASTENERS OR
ZIPPER.

FOLD

SEAMED SIDE TO
ACCOMMODATE OTHER
HALF OF FASTENER OR
ZIPPER. OUTSIDE STITCHING
EDGE SLIDES UNDER FLANGED
STRIP TO FASTEN.
THREE INCH STRIP OF DUCK
FOLDED AND SEWN BETWEEN
LINING AND DUCK, HALF OF
LENGTH TO ACCOMMODATE
FASTENERS ACROSS THE BOTTOM
HALF OF BAG.

FOLD

the filler shifts as happens with all sleeping bags I've ever seen, there's a trick to getting it back in place. Just spread the opened bag inside up on a clean grassy area, cut a limber switch, and beat the bag methodically from bottom to top, redistributing its filler.

HOMEMADE HEATER

Heaters made of metal gasoline and oil drums stand up under roaring fires for decade after decade throughout the northern parts of the continent. The large chunks of wood they accommodate make them particularly functional.

There is often a cold-chisel artist in the locality "back of beyond" who will adapt such a big metal barrel for a few dollars. Or, you can do it yourself. The final stove can be made presentable enough for the swankiest cabin or lodge, especially after bright aluminum paint is applied.

"All you need," says our friend William H. Carter, "is a gas barrel, a hammer and chisel, and a big chew of tobacco."

In the last one Bill converted for me, however, he pressed several other

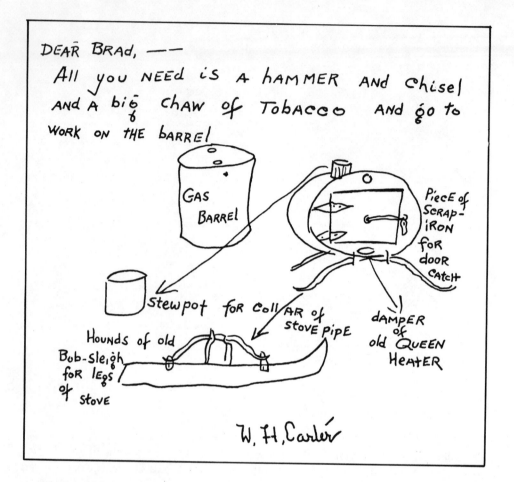

DEAR BRAD, ——
All you NEED is A hAMMER ANd Chisel ANd A big ChAw of TobAcco ANd go to woRk oN THE bARREl

GAS BARREl

PiEcE of SCRAp-iRoN foR dooR cAtCh

Stewpot foR collAR of stovE pipE

HoundS of old Bob-sleigh foR legs of stovE

dAmpER of old QuEEN HEAtER

W. H. Carter

widely assorted items into service as his own drawing shows. If the particular gadgets this ex-Mountie adapted hadn't been at hand, you may be certain he would have nonchalantly substituted something else.

It's sort of like the case of the camp cook on a Canadian geographical survey party that Dr. W. H. McLearn of Ottawa took into British Columbia's Peace River country near our homestead the other summer.

"Now where is that blasted, cussed, ding-danged . . . ? Oh, to blazes with it. This will do!" Dr. McLearn, who's still wondering what he really ate that night, heard this cook sputtering.

STOVE-PIPE STOVE

You can make yourself a tin-can stove, as shown in the drawing. Another trappers' favorite, because of the inexpensive ease with which a string of overnight cabins can be provided with warmth, it goes one step further and utilizes stove pipe in similar fashion.

Join two sections of knock-down seven-inch pipe so as to make a single fourteen-inch cylinder. Unless the cabin has a dirt floor, set this in a box of sand or loam. Brace it with several rocks.

Four-inch pipe can be elbowed out of the top rear of the cylinder. Wire supports are generally improvised to steady this smoke vent.

A flattened section of pipe, bent at the edges to fit the top of the stove more snugly, forms a lid that can be lifted for fueling. This is sometimes loosely hinged with wire or with metal clips cut on the spot. An air hole is ordinarily punched in the top.

Make four or more cuts with a can opener or ax, pie-wedge fashion, in the lower front of the cylinder. Push these flaps outward to accommodate, for instance, a small baking powder tin open at both ends. Care should be taken to clinch this can securely in place. The lid of the small container can then control the draft.

Some bushwackers use a second push-on cover punctured with nail holes for medium draft, proving that you can revel in every comfort of home just by exercising the little grey cells.

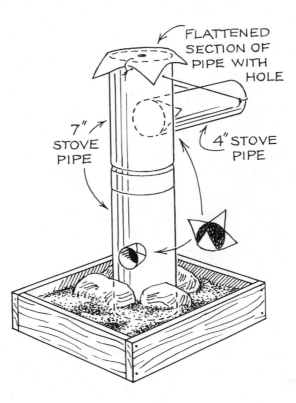

FLATTENED SECTION OF PIPE WITH HOLE

7" STOVE PIPE

4" STOVE PIPE

5

Camp Furniture

CAMP BED

You can make your own camp bed, actually a sort of trapper's cot, by sewing together substantial canvas, seven feet long and four feet wide, with a four-inch tubular seam running along each long side. You just cut and smooth two poles to insert in these tubes. Then reset the pole ends on a log or stone at each end of the cot to keep body and bedding off the ground.

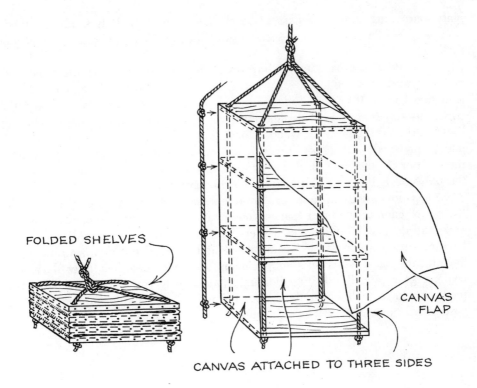

FOLDED SHELVES

CANVAS FLAP

CANVAS ATTACHED TO THREE SIDES

TENT SHELVES

Bore holes in each corner of several squarish shelves, space these shelves by knots on four suspended ropes, and hang the whole contrivance by a single rope at the top. You can tack canvas around three sides of this arrangement and have a canvas flap opening and closing handily at the front.

CAMP CHEST

For packing and keeping outdoor equipment in one place, ready to pick up and stow in or atop the car when that next camping exodus pleasantly arrives, there's nothing like a large chest which you can keep padlocked. Needs will vary, of course, so all such lockers will be somewhat different in size and shape.

The basic idea is to divide such a lockable box into convenient compartments and to fit the whole thing with handles. It makes a compact arrangement for those many necessary small odds and ends like needle and thread, blanket pins, sharpening stone, compasses, matchcases, and such. It is similar to those compact, drop-in type drawers seen in print shops and in newspaper composing rooms.

To build a compartmented box from the ground up, assemble what you need to carry in as compact an arrangement as you can manage. Then design a container to fit. It's a sound idea to make a dummy cardboard box first, sticking partitions and shelves in with tape until you get them properly spaced, then to duplicate everything in plywood. Good for the purpose is exterior 5/6-inch marine plywood, with brass screws to prevent rusting. Use thinner plywood for the interior if you want, and don't forget to allow for the fact that even then the plywood is likely to be thicker than the cardboard.

Keep possessions in units or containers as much as possible. For example, the motor camper will find that a wooden box about 3 feet long and 1½ feet wide and deep will hold stoves, lantern, flashlight, and camp ax. All you'll then have to do when you reach a campsite at night is haul out this box, and you'll have all the basic items for pitching camp and getting supper after dark. The cooking gear can all ride together in a packsack if you wish. The perishable food, of course, will be in the icebox. Nonperishable food can be carried in pasteboard boxes that you'll later burn.

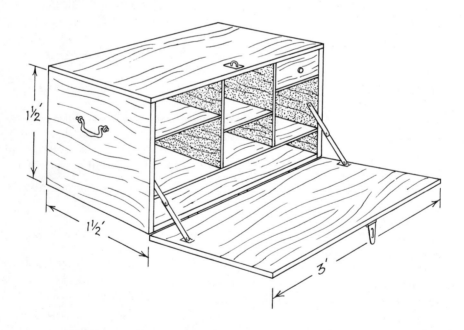

4-PLATES

4-LEGS
12-SCREWS

CHEST/TABLE

Dr. E. Russel Kodet has extended his screw-in idea to tables. Specifically, the top of his camping chest is removable and boasts leg sockets under each inside corner. When he is in camp and ready for this bit of furniture, all he has to do is screw in four 8-inch legs which he's packed along in the camping box itself.

Such wooden legs, available at hardware stores for up to eighty cents each (depending on size and make), come with bolt projections that screw into a plate, itself screwed to the bottom insides of the four corners of what you're using for your own tabletop.

STOOL

Split a short log. Smooth the flat surface, using sandpaper if you want a really finished job. Take a brace and bit, an auger, or even a jackknife. Bore four holes in the underside as shown in the drawing.

Angle in four lengths of sapling or tree limb, about two inches in diameter, so that the finished stool will be eighteen inches high. The tops of these legs should be whittled until they fit snugly. For camp use, just drive them into place. For a cabin or lodge, fasten them with glue or slant small nails through them into the slab.

An effective touch, if you are taking pains, is to bore a small hole through the seat and into the top of each leg, then to secure the latter by hammering in

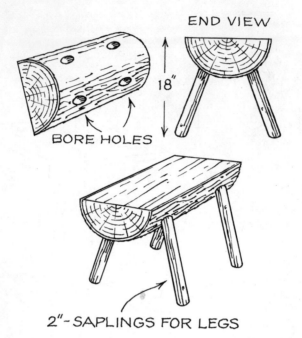

END VIEW

18"

BORE HOLES

2"-SAPLINGS FOR LEGS

a wooden peg. Softwood dowels will adapt themselves easily. Hardwood pegs have to be whittled with greater preciseness. Both will fit more solidly if first dipped in glue.

Waterproof glue in powder form is available for such furniture making. When prepared according to the particular instructions and applied thinly and evenly to smooth, tightly fitting joints, it may be counted upon to make a union stronger than the wood itself. Other satisfactory glues may be purchased at any hardware or variety store. Directions accompany them. Generally speaking, glued joints should be kept under pressure for some four hours and not subjected to strain for an additional twenty hours.

Stools so made often bring extraordinary prices at country auctions, under the guise of early American antiques.

TABLE WITH BENCHES

The simplest eating arrangement for camp, or even for the patio or backyard, is a table with benches attached. Six poles and several slabs will do the job, as the illustration shows. Make the tabletop about thirty inches high, the tops of the benches a foot lower.

Similar combinations are pleasantly inviting when put up around your home or lodge. Four long posts are first driven solidly into the ground, and the entire piece is constructed on these supports.

CATTAIL MAT

Who does not know these tall strap-leaved plants with their brown sausage-like heads which, growing in large groups from two to nine feet high, are exclamation points in wet places throughout the temperate and tropical countries of the world? Cattails are known in different places as rushes, cossack asparagus, cat-of-nine-tails, bulrushes, and flags. Sure signs of fresh or brackish water, they are tall, ruggedly stemmed perennials with stiff, thin, swordlike green leaves up to six feet long.

An easy way to make rush mats for home use or for sale is to tie together the butts of three dried and then briefly water-soaked cattail leaves, then to braid them in the usual manner. Once a rush starts to taper, lay in the thicker end of another, continuing the two as one strand. This way the braiding can be continued as long as you want. Rush mats can then be made by winding and sewing the flat coil together to the size desired.

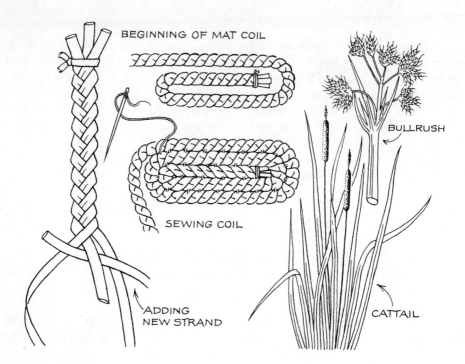

BEGINNING OF MAT COIL

SEWING COIL

ADDING
NEW STRAND

BULLRUSH

CATTAIL

CATTAIL BASKET

Braid your cattails as before and wind and sew the resulting flat coil together to make a basket bottom of the desired size. For the sides, continue to
coil and sew the braid flatly along the perimeter, one atop the other, as high
as you wish.

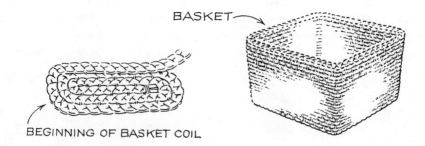

BASKET

BEGINNING OF BASKET COIL

6

Clothes and
Personal Items

PONCHO

One of the handiest pieces of rainy-weather trail gear is a poncho, and by making your own you can assure yourself of an extra ground cloth or tarp. You'll want a waterproof fabric, either sheet plastic or coated nylon. Seams can then be cemented or sewn. If sewn, these joinings should be coated with a rubber cement to make them waterproof.

A sheet 5 feet long and 3½ feet wide, folded in the middle, will give you excellent protection, all the better because of the fine ventilation afforded by such a garment. If two of you will be traveling with each other and you alternate the ball and socket portions of the snaps, your two ponchos can be fastened together to make a larger tarp or ground cloth—for which provision

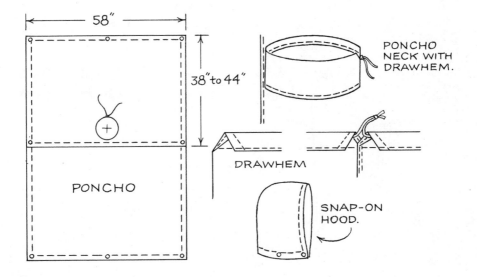

58"

38" to 44"

PONCHO

PONCHO NECK WITH DRAWHEM.

DRAWHEM

SNAP-ON HOOD.

you should set grommets at the corners and midway along each side. The drawing shows where the snaps should go.

There must be a neck hole, of course. This you can effectively close when you are using the poncho as a tarpaulin if you'll add a sleeve, a bit more than half as high as the hole is wide, closed by a drawstring. This neck hole, not centered as you might expect, is best cut forward of the center fold of the poncho. If you'll likely be shouldering a large pack, advance the neck hole even more to accommodate this extra bulk and arrange the side snaps to fit.

CHAPS

The one disadvantage of wearing a poncho in stormy weather, other than its tendency to lift and swirl in a high wind, is the way moisture drips from it onto the legs. A rugged pair of chaps, which can be sewn of lightweight coated nylon, may therefore be well worth including in your outfit.

Fitting over the boots you'll be wearing, chaps slip over the legs, reaching to the crotch and, on the outside of the leg, several inches higher. There each can be attached to the belt by an easily adjusted lace.

What you'll really be making, of course, is a couple of individually fitting tubes, the very simple details of which are shown by the drawing. If you'd like the chaps to fit more snugly, just make them flatly open and set in snaps along each outer side.

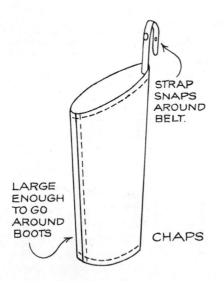

STRAP
SNAPS
AROUND
BELT.

LARGE
ENOUGH
TO GO
AROUND
BOOTS

CHAPS

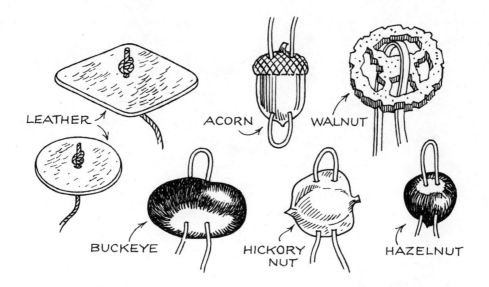

LEATHER   ACORN   WALNUT

BUCKEYE   HICKORY NUT   HAZELNUT

BUTTONS

To make harmonizing buttons for outdoor clothing, a bone of the desired circumference can be sawed into sections, then pierced with two small holes so it can be sewn to the garment. Sufficiently stiff leather, too, can be cut to size, pierced, and similarly used.

Then there are nuts. Smaller nuts, such as dried acorns, can be pierced with two small holes and used intact. With something such as a tiny hickory nut, husk and dry it first. Bigger nuts, such as wild walnuts, can be sawed into ¼-inch sections, smoothed with fine sandpaper, and varnished. These already boast their own holes for sewing.

The drawings tell the rest of the story.

GAUCHO BUTTON

Here's a particularly attractive and serviceable button of another sort, so rugged that the hard-riding gauchos of South America used to hook one between their first two toes in place of a stirrup.

There are two ways to make this type of fastener. For the simpler, just take a strip of leather, say one-half to an inch wide, and taper it to a point. About 1½ inches back from this point, cut a horizontal slit as long as the leather is wide. Wet the leather, turn the point inward and draw it through the slit, tighten, and the button is complete.

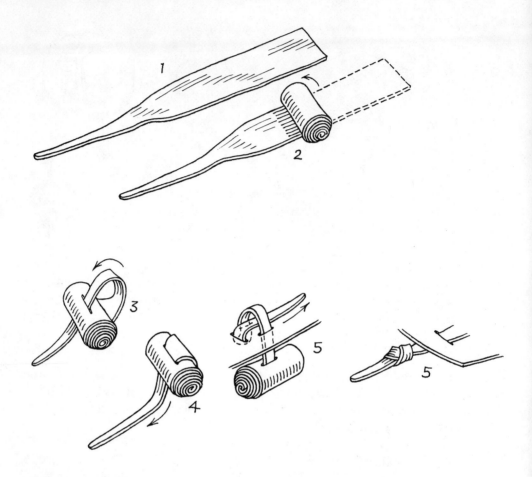

For a larger and more picturesque leather button, again taper a short piece of leather, damper it, and roll it tightly from the wider end. Once about two-thirds of its length is rolled, make a slit through the roll, pass the tip through this, and draw tight.

Incidentally, the end of the leather strip that protrudes from such finished buttons can be shoved up and back through two slits in an article, then pushed back in through a third hole and fastened under its own snug loop.

CONCHAE

To fasten your leather conchae to bridles, saddles, and other outdoor equipment—thus holding two or more parts together—first cut a smooth or zigzag-edged leather disk large enough to cover the holes by which the equipment parts are to be attached. This is your concha.

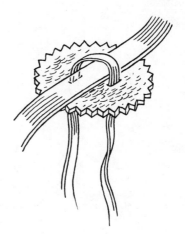

Then take a narrow leather or rawhide strip and, near the middle, cut two slits in this, parallel to its length, leaving just enough space between the pair to go through the parts that are to be held together. Draw the strip through the holes in the two or more items, then pass one end through the slit in its other length. To hold this initial fastening in place, just tighten the other end through the slit in the length just engaged. It's simpler than it sounds, as shown by the drawing.

TANNING LEATHER

Why waste the skin of that fairly won animal, particularly when so many memory-enticing practicalities can be made from it? If you have just downed a deer and are camping in one spot, for example, here's a simple way to turn the hide into usable leather.

Skin the trophy carefully, taking care to nick the hide as little as possible. Continue to use a sharp knife. Now working over your knee, if you find that easiest, remove as much flesh and fat as you can. Then weigh the skin down in water for several days, until patches of hair slip out when you give them an easy tug.

Lay the hide on a smooth log. Scrape one side and then the other, removing both hair and grain. Many consider it best to complete this process in one operation, before the skin dries. It can be redampened, however. By driving the point of your longest knife into an easily clasped block of wood, you can provide an additional hold for manipulating the graining instrument with both hands.

When the job of removing the hair and grain is completed, the moist hide may be thoroughly rubbed in a mixture of the animal's fat and brains, which

have been simmered together in equal amounts. The hide should be allowed to remain in this state for several days. Then it should be washed as clean as possible. Wring it as well as you can, perhaps by rolling it loosely around two poles that are lying parallel on the ground, then turning these in opposite directions.

The skin must then be pulled, rubbed, and stretched while drying if you do not want it to become stiff. If you plan to use it for footwear, however, rigidity may be a virtue.

The hide finally may be smoked by hanging it well away from the campfire for a few days, within reach of fumes but not of heat. Or, you can make a special smudge with green or rotten wood, taking the same precautions regarding heat. The sweet, oily smoke produced by burning green birch achieves a particularly pleasing effect.

MAKING RAWHIDE

Rawhide is prepared more easily. For this you can dry the green skin in the shade, at odd moments scraping the fleshy side as bare as possible with any dull instrument, such as a piece of rock or bone flattened on one side. In my own small collection, I have an ancient Indian-made jade scraper, shaped like a tomahawk head, that works fine.

The skin may be conveniently held by stretching the portion that is being worked across the knee. Or, like many of us, you may prefer to leave it tacked or pegged to some smooth surface, such as under the eaves on the north side of a shed, where jays and other hungry birds will aid your efforts.

If you want your rawhide to be soft, you probably will have to wet the fleshy side, allow it to dry, and then rescrape the skin, doing this as many times as may be necessary until it is satisfactorily pliable.

Care must be taken not to dampen the other side if retention of hair or fur is desired. If the hair or fur is too long, it may be clipped. If you want it off entirely, this can be accomplished by wetting the coat until it starts to loosen, whereupon you can scrape it off in great clumps.

BONE
SCRAPER

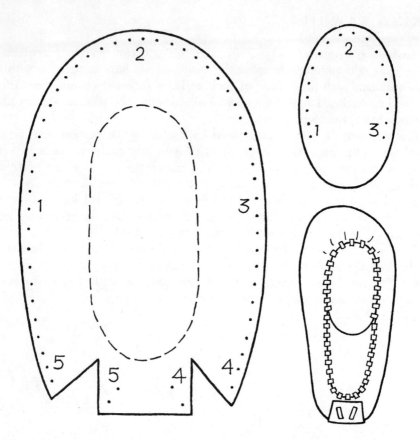

MOCCASINS

If you have animal skins, you can make moccasins. You can also fashion similar moccasins from such fabrics as blankets, but except in an emergency these will seldom wear long enough to merit the trouble. Nor are excessively fragile hides, such as rabbit, customarily worth bothering with for footwear.

Soft, tanned leather is an easily worked and comfortably light material for moccasins, but it soon wears out in wet and rough going. In such localities as the log-cabin country of the continental Northwest where this type of foot covering is popular, the common practice is to protect moccasins from dampness with store rubbers and overshoes.

For a more enduring moccasin, which will also give the feet better protection, it is best especially under rugged conditions to use as stiff and tough a chunk of hide as possible. In preparing the green skin, you should not take any steps to soften it. Not only should you not tan it, but you should scrape it only enough to smooth any irregularities that might hurt the feet. The hair can be left facing inward.

One moccasin pattern which is as practical as it is simple is shown by the accompanying illustration. You can fit this pattern to your size by standing on the material to be used, or on a more easily manipulated paper sample, and drawing an oval around the foot. Do not attempt to trace closely to the ends of the toes, in order to allow sufficient room for free movement.

You can then add about three inches all around for the tops of the moccasins. Or, if you have plenty of leather, you may want to bring these sides high around the ankle Indian-fashion in two flaps, which can be tied by wrapping them with several turns of lacing.

A way to save work in the beginning is by making a trial moccasin from, preferably, a comparably thick piece of fabric. These can be used later as linings or as indoor slippers.

Once the sections of the moccasin are cut, punch or slit holes around the edges as shown in the drawing. Thongs can be easily made from odd bits of leather by cutting them around and around, as we'll consider in a moment. Such thongs, or some other lacing, should be run through the holes to join the parts as marked.

SPECIAL MOCCASIN SOLE

The old plains Indians wore soles on their moccasins and today so do many of the dwindling numbers of mountain men in the Northwest, including those who live near our log-cabin home in northern British Columbia. For these soles,

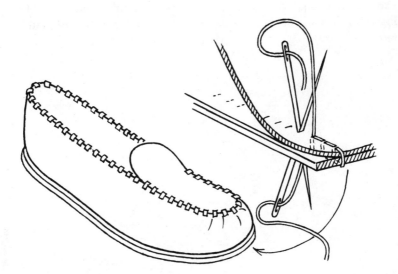

buckskin cut to fit will do. Although these days many use heavy nylon thread for the sewing, rawhide or sinew thongs were once commonly employed to stitch the soles to the footwear. Suit yourself.

Whenever the sole wears through, put on a new one. These soles last from three days to a week in heavy going, depending on the weather and the amount of travel. Native-type moccasins, outfitted with them, can be depended upon to last over a month.

Incidentally, such homemade leather moccasins worn with two pairs of woolen socks are the most perfect footwear imaginable for high, dry country. When the slippery snows come, however, one can break his fool neck wearing them. Native moccasins, in any event, are then still most delightful to change into when you come back to camp after a day afield. And even in the biggest city, their unforgettable woodsy odor, imparted by hours of tanning over smoky fires, takes one back to the sort of small, bright campfire you get going in the wilderness at dusk.

LACING

A thong or lace can be swiftly cut from an old moccasin top or odd piece of rawhide. If you have a sharp knife, one method is to find a smooth log with a stub or branch sticking up for use as a guide. A nail or peg will also serve for this purpose.

Suppose you want a lace ¼ inch thick. First, round any square edges from the leather. Second, start the first 1 or 2 inches of lace by severing a narrow strip of the correct width from the sheet.

Now come the mechanics. Using a billet of wood, tap your sharp knife, point first, into the log so the blade is facing away from you ¼ inch from the projection. Then place the started lace between this guide and the knife. By pulling the lace and turning the leather, you will automatically cut around and around, manufacturing as long a thong as there is material.

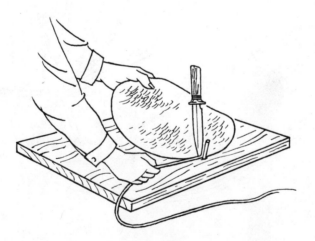

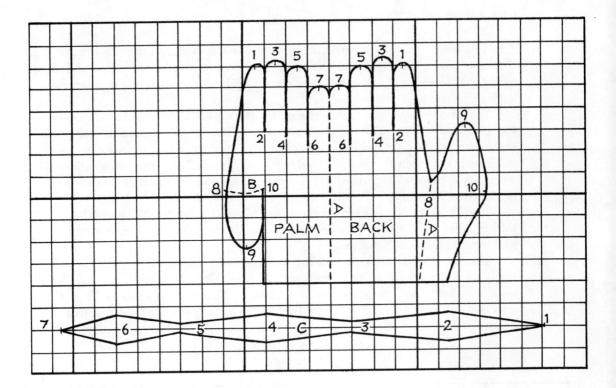

LEATHER GLOVES

Making your own gloves is a lot easier than it looks, if you sew with a sharp needle and strong buttonhole thread, waxing the thread so that it won't pull too much while you're working.

Using a soft pencil, draw the pattern for one hand on the back side of your leather. Next, turn the material over and trace the other hand on an unoccupied spot.

If you wish the gloves to close with snaps, cut each vent in the center of the inside, hem it, and then reinforce the material around the fasteners with small scraps of leather. When you buy the snaps, perhaps at a hobby or dressmakers' store, secure the necessary tool for setting them in. Buttons may be used instead.

In the pattern shown here, fold "A" up and fold "B" down. The strip at the bottom is the glove gusset, which fits in between the fingers to provide freedom of action.

LEATHER MITTS

Any leather mitts you make for wilderness use will be more satisfactory if they extend high enough to shield the particularly vulnerable wrists and if their tops fit sufficiently close to exclude snow and debris which might otherwise necessitate frequent removals.

Too, if you have had much reason to use mitts in the woods and fields, you have probably found it as handy as I have to have a slit made in the palm of one and a sewed-on flap added to cover that opening when it is not in use. With such a mitt on the master hand, you can quickly bare your trigger finger whenever it becomes expedient, for example, when you see the hulking darkness of that massively antlered bull moose.

The drawing tells the rest of the story. Match the letters. When joining A, pucker to fit. At B, sew in stretched elastic or, if you prefer, add a drawstring to give you a means of tightening.

There's a handy trick to wearing such mitts in cold open country. Sew a thong or other lacing to the wrist ends of the mitts that, worn around the neck, will hold them suspended at waist length. That way you're less likely to lose one, an accident that, in really frigid circumstances, might mean a frozen hand.

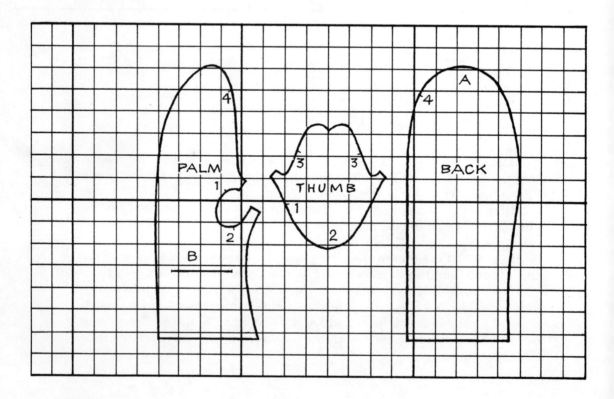

TUBING FOR STOCKINGS

The simple but all-important formula for comfortable wilderness walking is heavy socks and big shoes. Regardless of heat, cold, or moisture, only wool socks are suitable for long treks. These socks may vary from thin to medium during the summer, and from medium to heavy during the frosty months.

When you want to cut down on weight in the woods, here's a trick that'll save time, space, and ounces. Knit, or have made for you, woolen tubing similar to elongated stocking legs. All you'll then have to do is tie pieces of string around the bottoms of two such tubes and draw them on like ordinary stockings.

When what amounts to the heel of one tube wears through, standard operating procedure is to twist it around so that the hole is over the instep. By turning the tube, you can wear each stocking in four different positions without mending. Nor is that all. Finally, just cut off the entire section that has served as the foot, retie your string, and begin the whole process anew.

TIE RING

When I was first learning knots in the old seacoast town of Beverly, Massachusetts, under the tutorage of the old sailor who was our scoutmaster, Johnny Lee culminated his teachings with the Turk's head—which, if tied with a stiff cord or thong, will keep its hollowness for use as a kerchief ring or as a napkin holder for camp or lodge.

Although for final use you'll likely want to tie the Turk's head around a pole or similar object of the desired diameter, your first efforts may well be over two fingers of your left hand. For the basic knot, of which there are a number of variations, begin as if making a clove hitch. Instead of pushing the working end under the crossing, however, go over this and under the first turn. Press the first turn under the second. Then pass the working end over the second and under the first turn, as illustrated.

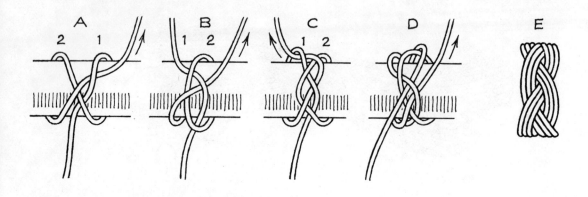

This is the nucleus of the notable Turk's head. When you are tying this in a small ring, bring the working end in beside the starting end and follow alongside the previous pattern for the traditional three times. If your material is thin, in relation to the object it is to encircle, the encirclements may be repeated to increase the size of the knot. But you should always end with a complete set of turns, bringing the working end to the left at the finish. The drawings show how easy all this actually is.

BELT

By salvaging or purchasing a buckle, you can use a strip of leather to provide yourself with a rugged and mystifying belt or, in a shorter length, with an attention-getting fob for your outdoor pocketwatch or pedometer. What you'll finish up with, that is, is a flat, triple plait made in three endless strands.

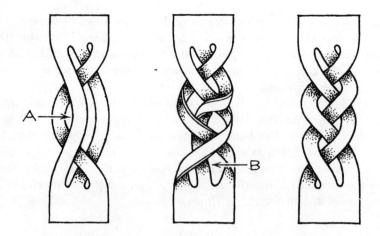

Once you've slit your leather strap, begin from the top as if working with three separate strips. The problem, of course, comes in eliminating the tangle which twists together at the bottom. To help achieve this, make the first plaits as tight as possible to give you more working room. Loosen them later.

Cross the right over the center strand, as shown in the drawing, then the left over the right. Holding the leather in this position, shove the bottom entirely through gap A, leaving the strips twisted. If you'll now pass the bottom through gap B, everything will be smooth once more.

These actions—each side strip moving to the opposite side and back again, and the center strip shifting to both sides in turn—will be enough for the short piece of leather you'll need for a job. When you're plaiting a belt though, you can repeat the process as many times as feasible. Just be sure the original strap is a third longer than what you finally want, to make up for the length used by braiding.

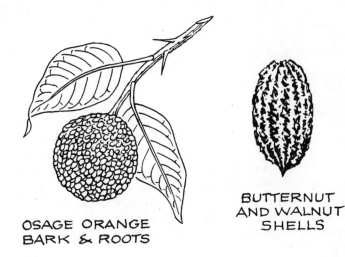

OSAGE ORANGE
BARK & ROOTS

BUTTERNUT
AND WALNUT
SHELLS

NATURAL DYES

The making of varicolored cushions will brighten the log cabin or lodge and make it more comfortable. Just sew two pieces of fabric, the size you want, together on three sides while they are inside out. Add a zipper to the fourth side perhaps, and then turn. Native fillers such as wild marsh hay, aromatic evergreen needles, and soft sphagnum moss may be used to make these invitingly plump.

You may even like to experiment with natural dyes. Cloth immersed in liquid in which swamp maple bark has been boiled will come out a mountain-lake blue. To make it a professional job, you need only add a little iron sulphate to the solution first. If there is none in the vicinity, a dime's worth may be pur-

WILD
SUNFLOWER
BLOSSOMS

SWAMP MAPLE
BARK

chased from a drugstore. Or, you may obtain it from a cobbler's shop where it is known as copperas.

Alder bark, when boiled, gives off a tawny yellow dye that has colored many an Indian's garments. The rich hue of pioneer homespuns was often obtained by boiling the outer nut shells and the inner bark of the butternut tree. Wild sunflower blossoms contain a sunny stain that has the exciting hue of gold; so do goldenrod flowers, and the bark and roots of the Osage orange.

SUNGLASSES

Snowblindness is caused by the exposure of the unprotected eyes to glare from the snow. It can occur on cloudy days and in tents. Prevention is the best answer. Don't wait until your eyes hurt to wear your sunglasses.

A primitive "sunglass," particularly fine for the purpose, is a piece of wood, bone, leather, or other material with narrow eye slits cut in it. These and similar eyeshades prove to be surprisingly excellent in blizzards because the slits can be kept clean by brushing them off, whereas regular glasses may give trouble by frosting. Such protection is also effective in the deserts of the world.

You may be amazed to find that you can see quite well through the small slits without prescription glasses. This intrigued my woodsman friend, C. B. Colby, with whom I wrote *The Art and Science of Taking to the Woods,* so

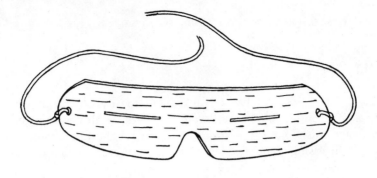

Bill experimented with holes he made in paper and cardboard. He discovered he could read small print without any lens at all when he looked at it through a tiny hole held close to the eye. The smaller the hole, the better it worked. Using this method, he could easily read the small print of maps and compass bearings.

An oculist gave a simplified explanation for this. He said that when an individual's eyesight is imperfect, rays which do not enter the exact center of the eyeball are distorted unless corrected with glasses. By peeping through a pinhole, you reduce the rays entering the eye to those in the very middle of the eye lens. If you lose or break your prescription glasses, then make a substitute pair by punching tiny holes in paper or birch bark with a needle or pointed stick.

WILDERNESS TOOTHBRUSH

A small green twig, chewed to a pulpy consistency at one end, will serve as a wilderness toothbrush. Or you can pound the tip of a small green stick between two stones until it is fibrous and use that. Soap, salt, and baking soda all are good substitutes for toothpaste.

SPLINT

Find a birch tree that has a trunk about the size of the injured limb and strip off a sufficiently wide circumference of bark. With dry sphagnum moss for padding, bind this around the arm or leg. Such a light and comfortable covering will give a surprising amount of support until you can get to a doctor.

BIRCH
BARK AND
SPHAGNUM
MOSS

Cooking Gear

7

OUTDOOR COOKING TOOLS

Grilling over open embers still gives you the tastiest food in the world, not that there aren't tricks to all trades. With steaks, for instance, the secret is to get a glowing bed of lasting hardwood coals started, then scatter on a few chips and shavings. These will flare up enough to give the meat that favorful char enjoyed by so many.

You can even let the outdoors furnish some of your cooking tools. For example, all the equipment you need for baking bread is a long green stick, preferably peeled, with several branch stubs remaining. Just make a somewhat stiff bannock dough. Wind this on the stick and then implant its sharpened end at an angle near the coals—all as described in detail in my *Wilderness Cookery*.

The drawings of this and other outdoor cooking tools are pretty much self-explanatory. The Ojibways, for instance, used to make drinking cups by folding a thin sheet of birch bark as shown and holding the resulting cone in place by inserting the folded portion in a split green stick. If the tension of

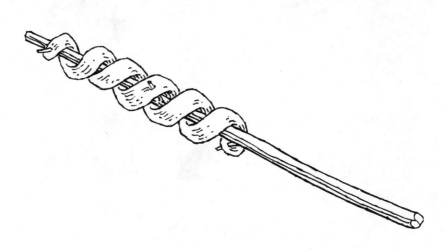

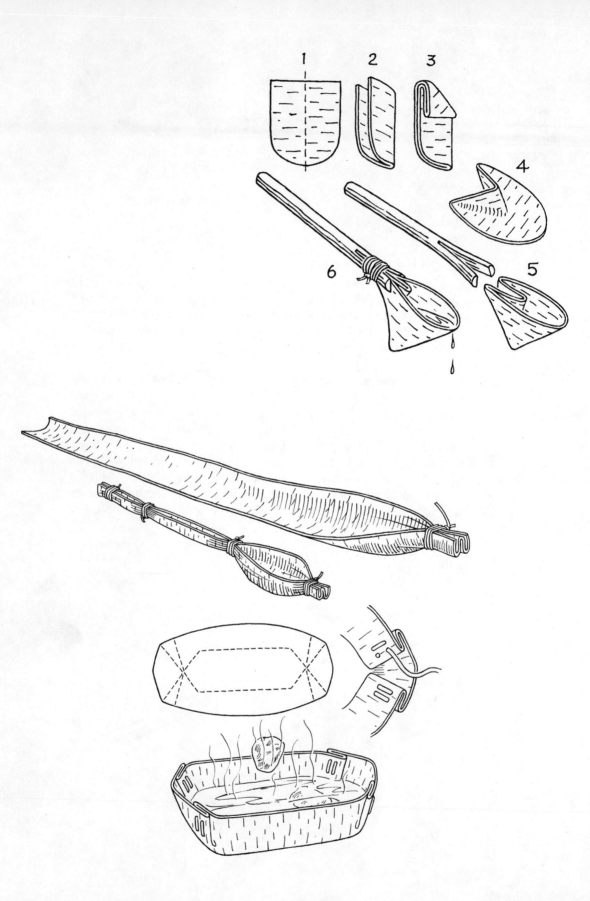

this is not sufficient, the cleft can be lashed together by some woodland fiber such as tough little spruce roots.

Then there is a simple birch bark spoon which will be easier to manufacture if you first make both bark and bindings more pliable by soaking them in hot water. For your plate, any clean bark flat will serve. For suspending your tea pail on a green crosspiece, stretched over the fire across forked green sticks, invert the natural crotch of a sapling with a notch cut in its longer end to hold the wire handle.

Do you know how to boil water in a birch bark container? Make container as shown, by folding a smooth rectangle of bark and holding each end with an inserted twig or thorn. Dropping in hot clean stones will turn the trick. Or, quicker, set the water-filled kettle on the coals, blanketing the fire with heaped ashes so that no flames can curl up the sides. If fire does not touch the bark above the water line, it will not burn.

GRILL

One of the more knowledgeable and enthusiastic younger woodsmen I know is E. Russel Kodet, M.D., with whom I wrote *Being your own Wilderness Doctor* and *The Home Medical Handbook*. When he can find time away from a busy California practice, as he does periodically, my friend is usually off in

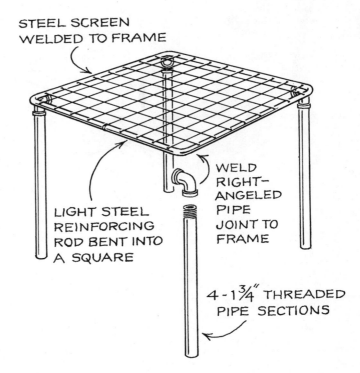

STEEL SCREEN WELDED TO FRAME

WELD RIGHT-ANGELED PIPE JOINT TO FRAME

LIGHT STEEL REINFORCING ROD BENT INTO A SQUARE

4-1¾" THREADED PIPE SECTIONS

the mountains with his wife, Shirley, for whose fine campfire cooking activities he has designed a portable grill.

This grill has one refinement that makes it different from the fixed, folding-leg grill I have carried for years, and this is screw-in legs. Dr. Kodet made his grill by bending a light steel reinforcing rod into a square. At each of the corners he welded a right-angled pipe joint. When he is on the spot, all he has to do is screw in the four lengths of the 1¾-inch pipe that form the legs.

Light steel screening, welded across the top of this frame, provides a diamond-shaped meshwork that fairly begs for a brace of plump, sizzling steaks or array of gleaming trout.

LIGHTWEIGHT GRILL

You can go one step farther and make the illustrated grill, which will work even better if the tips of the four legs are sharpened with a file. If you keep each of these supports about one-foot long, you'll allow yourself enough room underneath for the sort of small fire that's best for wilderness cooking.

Such tiny blazes save time, especially if you're high in the mountains or deep in the tundras such as this continent's Land of Little Sticks, where the caribou roam below the Arctic Circle. They best utilize the limited amount of twigs and roots available for warmth.

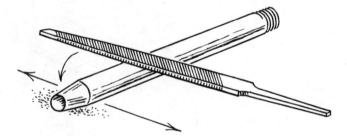

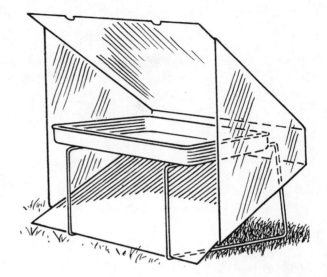

REFLECTOR BAKER

Half of a five-gallon can—one cut diagonally apart from top to bottom—makes a fine little reflector oven, with the addition of a shelf to hold what you're baking before the high blazing fire in front. Supports for a middle shelf can be snipped from wire coat hangers and inserted through holes punched in the oven's center. These will hold the shelf flat when the baker is tilted in position on one edge, as shown in the drawing. The shelf can be sheared from the remaining half of the can.

So, with a little effort and some ingenuity, you can make your next camp more enjoyable, and have fun manufacturing gear at the same time. The reflector baker in particular is one of the more useful refinements for outdoor gourmet cooking.

CHARCOAL STOVE

On this young continent even city dwellers live close to their wilderness background. The glowing embers of the all-night campfire continue to be part of America's pioneer heritage, although today they are more often found in the home's charcoal burner. Expensive equipment for a burner, over which steak will appetizingly sizzle and fresh trout flake, is not necessary. You can easily make a functional charcoal stove for yourself with no more than one large can, a punch-type can opener, and a bit of wire, by following the drawing.

To use this functional little stove outdoors in your yard or inside on the fireplace hearth, start with a small foundation fire of paper, wood, and other handy flammables. Feed small twigs or such until you have a brisk blaze. Then drop on a few small pieces of charcoal or, if you have them on hand, gradually add larger pieces. Swing stove by the wire handle outdoors or blow at the base indoors to make the fire burn more brightly.

DOUBLE BOILER

By similarly converting two cans of different sizes you can even provide yourself with a double boiler, a convenient contrivance lacking in most light-weight kits of nested cooking utensils. The drawing tells the story.

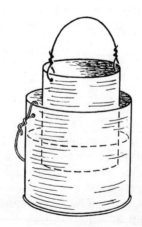

TEA KETTLE

What often remains most fondly in our minds after a wilderness trip are the memories of crackling twigs that boil the tea water at noon. The northern woodsman, particularly the Canadian, must sip his steaming cup of tea at the noon hour, even if he has nothing to eat. This is almost a religion up under the aurora borealis, and it's called "b'iling the kittle." Only a temporary fire is needed, a mere handful of dry wood that will flare up briefly and as quickly fall to ashes, a few of which invariably seem to swirl up to float unheeded in the hot, dark brew.

Get the water bubbling. Drop in a roughly measured teaspoon of tea for each cup of fluid and set immediately off the heat, in a safe place. Five minutes of steeping is sufficient.

You'll need your "kittle," though, and for this the home-made version is best. Get as large a can as you need—tomato-tin size if you're in the woods alone or one of the large fruit-juice containers for a small party. Take off the top of the can smoothly with a roll-around can opener. Then, just below the rim on opposite sides, punch two tiny holes with a nail. Loop a pliable wire through these so that you can suspend your tea kettle in the flames on a slanted stick, and you're happily in business.

TOASTER

Nothing tastes better than steak or fresh salmon broiled over the glowing coals of a hardwood campfire on a forked, green stick. However, there's often the difficulty that, over the heat necessary, the holder itself will burn before

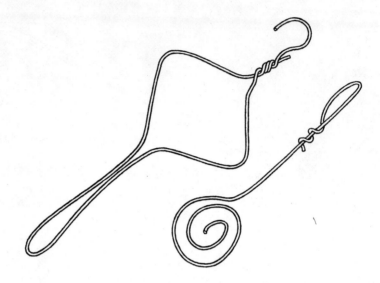

the meal is ready. By twisting (preferably unpainted) old coat hangers, you can provide yourself with a stabler support, as illustrated.

PLANK FOR A SALMON

This plank works with any fish. In each case you start with a heated, oiled, inch-thick birch or other hardwood plank or slab which can be hewn on the spot. The procedure works both indoors and out. I personally like it best with grilse.

A grilse, as you know, is the young of the salmon after its first return from the sea. A delectable way to serve these young Atlantic salmon is planked. I have enjoyed salmon prepared this way on the wild Half Moon of the southwest Miramichi River in New Brunswick and on the brawling Grand Cascapedia, which enhances Quebec's Gaspé Peninsula.

Start with your green wood plank or slab and, if you're going to be cooking before a campfire, nail or peg the opened and flattened fish to it so that it can be turned at every angle. Change positions as the cooking progresses.

First, wipe the cleaned and split grilse with paper or cloth toweling, rub inside and out with salt and black pepper in respective proportions of four to one and, if you're back in your kitchen, broil in a preheated oven at 450° for about twelve minutes or until flaky, basting with melted butter. Outdoors, as soon as the fish flakes beneath a testing twig it is ready to eat.

This procedure also brings out the flavor of steaks from freshly caught

salmon, from the north Pacific as well as the Atlantic, like no other method I've ever tried. Again, heat and oil the plank. Indoors, brown the steaks under the broiler for two minutes on each side. Then bake them in a 450° preheated oven for a few minutes more until they flake easily. Basting with melted butter will add to the flavor. Save that plank for the next time.

ALL-PURPOSE SHEET

The simplest and handiest thing to take along for general cooking and mixing purposes is a thin sheet of plastic, cut about two-feet square. This can be easily washed, quickly refolded, and conveniently carried from one wilderness area to another with a minimum of bother. Bark may be similarly

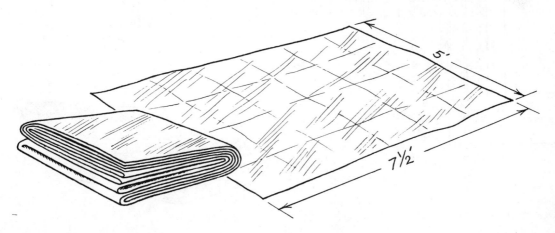

used, of course, but at best it's a nuisance. Foil or waxed paper is another answer for motorized campers, but you need a constant supply.

As a matter of fact, one of the most convenient items for each individual to carry when hiking, camping, skiing, fishing, canoeing, or otherwise enjoying himself out-of-doors is a thin sheet of lightweight plastic which you've cut to 5-by-7½-foot proportions. This will quickly fold into bandana-handkerchief size, small enough for the pocket of a sport shirt. It will then be with you, ready to be drawn over the head and shoulders as protection against storm, stretched amid the lower boughs of a tree for a rain shelter, spread on the ground as a dining cloth, pitched as a tarpaulin, and even used as a waterproof wrapping for that string of sleek trout.

KITCHEN-KNIFE CASE

Although large corks stuck on sharp fork tines will keep you from being jabbed when packing, kitchen knives need more protection. If you have long, slender carving knives, for instance, it is a simple matter to make functional wooden cases for them. Just take a piece of wood as long as each blade, or blade and handle if you prefer. Using a rip saw, cut a slot lengthwise in the piece deep enough to hold the complete blade. Cover the top of this slot with a thin bit of wood, and there you are.

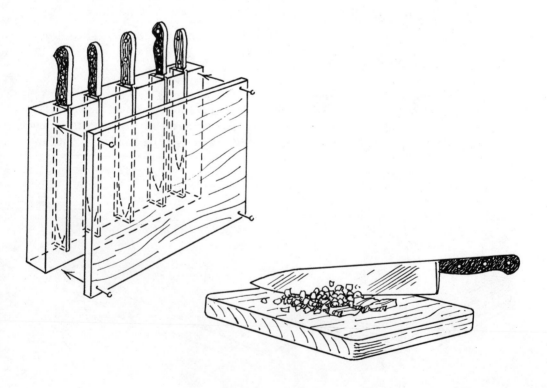

Make certain that the point of the knife is safely within the slot. Such cases can be fashioned for all types of carving, steak, and vegetable knives. You can fasten such wooden containers to the interior of your kitchen box. Then when you're ready to set out, you can tell if any knives are missing by checking the cases.

Incidentally, if there will be much slicing or chopping to do in camp, carry a clean square of soft pine on which to do it, instead of using a dulling plate or flat stone. Such a chopping block can be made to slide into one of your cabinet compartments, if you're motorized. The soft pine will protect the keen steel. Rinse and scour the wood after every use to eliminate odors.

FREE REFRIGERATION

Just about the first thing I do when occupying a new log cabin is to build cabinets for Vena and bookcases for both of us. If lumber is at hand, these can be put together in a very few minutes, as shown by the illustrations. Decide first on size. Assemble the four outer pieces. Then, perhaps using as a guideline the cans or books that are to be stored, mark on the inside of one of the sideboards the location of the shelves.

Nail on small strips to support these shelves. Do this, too, on the inside of the other sideboard. Fasten the frame together, nailing the sides inside the

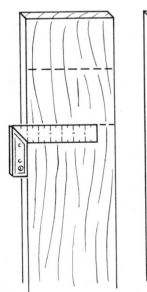

bottom and topboards for greater strength. Then set this frame in place against the wall, preferably nailing it there. Saw the shelves to measure and slide them into place, and eureka—storage space!

By building a small and lightweight version of one of these cabinets, screening the back, draping cheesecloth over the front, and suspending the whole thing by four cords ending in a single rope, you can provide a functional outdoor pantry. Hang this in a shady spot where it will be cooled by the breezes.

Want to cool it further? Then drape burlap or similar material over the front and back. Let the tops of this extend up over the box and keep them immersed there in a pan of water. Capillary action and evaporation will do the rest. During summers in the wilderness, you'll see survey parties using these to keep their meat and other perishables fresh.

Burlap-draped orange-crate coolers of this sort, suspended where breezes will speed evaporation, are frequently come upon in the desert. If water is in short supply, you can save some by placing a second pan beneath.

WILDERNESS REFRIGERATOR

At our cabin, and whenever we camp for any length of time beside water, we find one of the following refrigerators most functional. This can be any size desired, either a wooden box liberated from a store or one especially made of lumber or marine plywood. A handy size is 1 foot wide, 1½ feet deep, and 2 feet long. Use galvanized, aluminum, or brass nails to prevent rusting.

The refrigerator may have a simple hinged top, held from falling back by a short leather thong or, if small animals may bother by gnawing this, by a short brass chain. The shelves, if any, can be arranged any way you want. Or

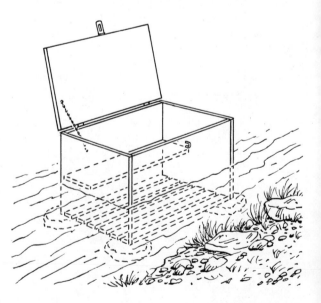

place canned goods on the slatted bottom, the contents of each marked by scratching or by using fingernail polish, as the labels will soon float off. The other items, if you use this in a stream whose water level fluctuates, can then be placed in covered pots that will float—a practice that we have long followed successfully at our British Columbia log cabin.

Locate this refrigerator close to the bank in a shady spot, set on stones if necessary, so that several inches of its bottom, where you've bored holes or arranged slats, will be immersed. If the whole box is made of slats, you'll need to flyproof the exposed portion with cheesecloth or screening.

ICE FOR CAMPING

Whenever it is possible, the automobile camper will find it's a good idea to freeze clean milk cartons full of water for use in the icebox. When this melts, you'll have some cold fresh water to drink, and the fluid won't be slushing around in the bottom of the box.

Speaking of perishables, you may find ice almost impossible to get at most campsites. So never pass up a chance to replenish your supply even if you still have a bit left. I've sewn together a piece of heavy, waterproof canvas to make a two-foot-square container, easily folded out of the way when not in use, in which to carry extra ice wrapped in newspapers. Admittedly, this will melt faster outside the icebox, but when the block in the box has melted partway down you'll probably have some left in your canvas container with which to replenish it. Just don't forget to empty the water periodically from the spare ice carrier so that it won't slop over at sudden stops.

8

Catching Food

MAKING A FISH LINE

You can make a line by unraveling a parachute suspension cord or similar cord or by twisting thread from cloths or plant fibers. A number of plants, such as nettles, are suggested in my two books on edible wild plants, *Free for the Eating* and *More Free-for-the-Eating Wild Foods*.

One way of making a line from the threads unraveled from your clothing, for instance, is to knot lengths of a half dozen or so at frequent intervals.

For a more scientific approach, fasten four threads at one end. Hold two threads in each hand. Roll and twist each of these double strands clockwise

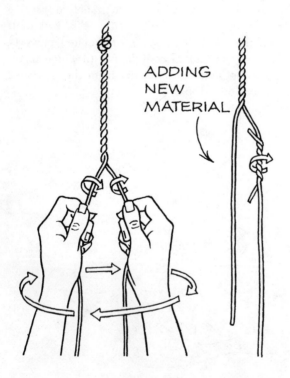

ADDING
NEW
MATERIAL

between thumbs and forefingers. At the same time, turn those in the master hand counterclockwise around those held in the other hand. Such twisting and winding must be done tightly, so that the completed line will not easily come apart.

Depending on the lengths of thread you are able to come by, end each of the four strands about two inches apart. This is to make the splicing on of the new strands more substantial. About an inch before any thread ends, twist on a new thread to continue the one just terminating.

Such an operation can be continued, so long as you have materials, to make a fish line of any length. If your quarry is more the size of a Dolly Varden, rather than Arctic grayling or rainbow trout, use a dozen or more strands for your line.

FISH HOOKS

In an emergency, you can cut your fish hooks from wood (preferably wood that is hard and tough). Whittle the shank first. Lash one or more sharp slivers to its lower end, so that they slant upward. You can even add a barb by tying, with thread unraveled from your clothing, another sliver even more acutely downward from the top. Large thorns, if available, can be utilized. Fish bones, too, will furnish both serviceable points and barbs.

One of the most primitive fishing devices, still used successfully if not always sportingly, is made by tying the line to the notched middle of a short piece of bone or wood that has been sharpened at both ends. Hidden in bait, this is swallowed by the fish, whereby a jerk of the cord pulls it crossways.

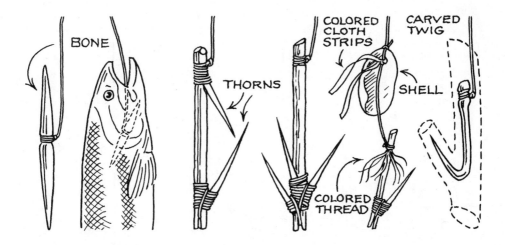

If you are ever desperate for food, gulls and other scavenger birds can be easily although unpleasantly caught by the same means—a device of this sort can be hidden in some bait such as decomposed fish. The other end of the line should be attached to something limber, such as a green sapling.

ICE FISHING

You can obtain fish in the winter, as every cold-climate sportsman knows, by angling through a hole in the ice. If you're camped nearby, you may want to keep this hole as open as possible until it is fished again. Cover it with brush or browse and heap loose snow atop that lid.

Fish tend to gather in deep pools, so try to cut your ice holes over the deepest parts of the lake or river. Place an easily fashioned rig, such as the one pictured, at several holes. When the bit of cloth that is serving as a signal flag moves to an upright position, pull up the fish and rebait the hook.

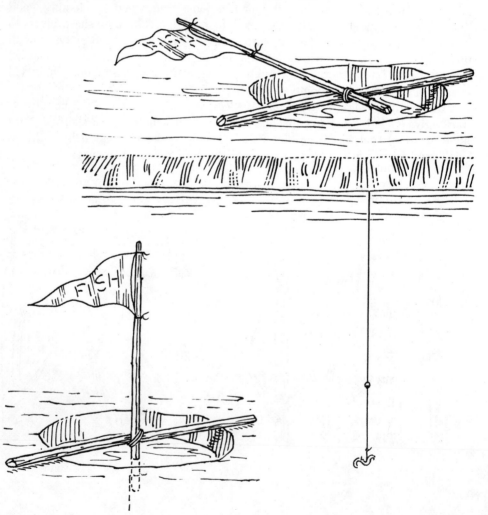

GILL NET

Freshly caught fish, when sufficiently fat and when not overcooked, will sustain you in top health for an unlimited period of time. They will, that is, if you can secure all you need to eat. The trouble with fish is that, with exceptions such as salmon, they're mainly lean and short in calories. A gill net may be your answer.

A gill net is one of the surest methods of catching fish, especially in still water such as near the inlet or outlet of a lake or in the back water of a large stream which you can block with this device. It can also be effectively used beneath the ice.

The way to go about making this, as shown by the illustration, follows. In a foodless emergency, particularly if you have just parachuted into the wilderness, a gill net can be made on the spot from the suspension lines and the core liners pulled from the insides of the chute.

1. Suspend a suspension-line casing, a line from which the core liner has been pulled, horizontally between something such as two trees at approximately eye level.

2. Hang an even number of core liners from this suspended line. These liners may be attached with a clove hitch or girth hitch, as shown, and spaced in accordance with the size mesh you desire. The smaller the mesh, the smaller the fish you can catch, while still entangling a large fish. One-inch spacing will result in a one-inch mesh, and so on. A good standard is a mesh of two and one-half inches.
The number of lines will be in accordance with the width, or length, of the net desired. If more than one man is going to work on this net, the length of the net should be stretched between the uprights. Then follow Step 8.

3. Start left or right. Skip the first line. Tie the second and third lines together with an overhand knot. Space according to the size mesh desired. Then tie 4 and 5, 6 and 7, and so on. One line will remain free at the end.

4. On the second row, tie 1 and 2 with the same simple overhand knot, 3 and 4, 5 and 6, and so on to the end.

5. For the third row, skip the first line and repeat Step 3 above.

6. For subsequent rows, repeat Step 4 and so on, according to the drawing.

7. As illustrated, you may want to use a guideline which can be moved down for each row of knots to ensure an equal-sized mesh. This is just another horizontal line tied to the two trees. Run this across the net

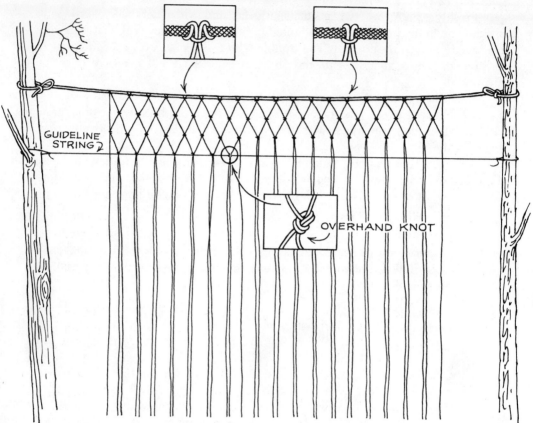

on the side opposite to the one you're working on, so that it will be out of the way.

8. When you have stretched the width between the uprights and approach ground level; move the net up by rolling it on a pole and continue until the net is the desired length.

9. When the gill net is completed, string a suspension-line casing along the sides to strengthen it and to make the setting of it easier.

10. Attach several wooden floats to the top of the net and stone anchors along its bottom

You can set this net across a stream, at right angles to the shore and preferably blocking the current, by using a pole as illustrated. The anchor line tightens the net into place. Incidentally, you'll occasionally have the additional feast of birds, caught while trying to steal a fish.

In winter, set the net by cutting holes in the ice of a lake or river. Using a pole slightly longer than the distance between the holes, attach a line to one end. Starting at the first hole, float the pole to the second hole and then on to the last hole where it is removed from the water.

Tie the net securely to the end of the line and pull the net under the ice until it is set, several inches below the ice to keep it from freezing. Make sure that the line is tied to both ends of the net to ease the work of checking and resetting.

BOLA

If survival ever becomes a problem, you can generally arm yourself with a bola, a primitive missile consisting of stones or other weights attached to the ends of thongs or even strips of clothing. Although the Spanish people are generally thought of in connection with the bola, Eskimos use a device of this sort consisting of several cords, each about a yard long with a small weight at the outer extremity.

The bola is grasped at the center from which all strings radiate, and the weights are twirled above the head. Hurled at flying birds, for example, the spinning strands often twist around one or more and bring them to the ground.

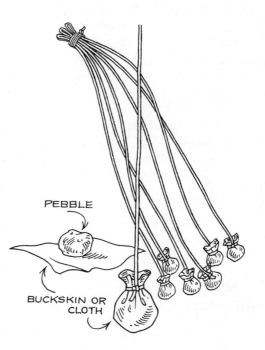

PEBBLE

BUCKSKIN OR CLOTH

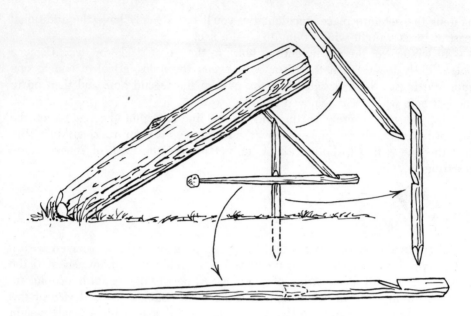

FIGURE-FOUR TRIGGER

For the capture of food animals in times of distress, the 300-year-old Hudson Bay Company recommends the use of deadfalls by any of its employees who may be stranded without adequate sustenance in the northern wilderness. The "Company of Adventurers'" pattern of the deadly figure-four trigger is very effective.

Essentially, you might prepare a deadfall by lifting one end of a heavy object such as a log. Prop this up with a stick, being sure to set the stick so insecurely that any animal or bird who moves the support will knock it loose. This you can encourage by affixing some bait to the prop. It's possible to go even further, arranging a few branches so that, to reach the bait, the victim will receive the full weight of the dislodged deadfall behind the shoulders.

SNARES

In a foodless emergency, even if you have a gun, you may wish to set a few snares, the principles of which are as simple as they are primitive.

KNIFE

For all his mastery of earth and space, man is a weak creature with inadequate teeth and without claws. He must rely on tools to perform many of the simplest functions and, since the earliest man picked up the first sharp-edged stone, the knife has been a primary tool in the wilderness. A man in the outdoors without a knife is a weakling, while the man with one is master of a hundred

situations. With the right kind of knife, you can warm yourself, feed yourself, shelter yourself, clothe yourself, and, if need be, defend yourself.

Here's the way W. D. Randall, Jr., whose hobby is making by hand the best outdoor knives in the world, says you manufacture one of your own. You can save fifty dollars or so and avoid a long wait.

There are no short cuts in the handcrafting of such fine blades. Therefore, you should go all the way and use only the best obtainable materials. Here, then, is the procedure.

1. Get a piece of carbon tool-steel knife stock.

2. Heat it cherry red and hammer out the rough blade in the general shape desired.

3. Grind the rough, forged blade to the size and shape of the desired blade.

4. Harden the blade by heating it cherry red and then immersing it in oil, tempering it. Draw out the brittleness and internal stresses by tempering the blade at low heat until it becomes a straw-blue color and can be cut with a new file.

5. Grind in lines, bevels, and contours and remove roughness.

6. Use a coarse hone and true up the cutting edge, removing any remaining waves and unevenness.

7. Regrind the blade on a fine-grit wheel to remove scratches made by the coarse hone.

8. Smooth the blade, first with coarse- and then with fine-grit emery cloth.

9. Polish the blade on a glue-up, coarse emery wheel.

10. Cut and shape the hilt from one-quarter-inch brass. Drill a hole and file it to rectangular shape to fit the handle tang. Fit hilt to the blade and solder in place.

11. Fit the handle to the tang, cutting rectangular holes in pieces of fiber, plastic, or leather. Slip into place and glue each separately. Drill a piece of one-half-inch duralumin for the butt and recess it to fit the tang. Drive it on tightly and peen it into place, or thread end of tang and use nut. When the glue is thoroughly dry, roughly shape the handle with a coarse file. Finish shaping with a finer file. Then smooth it, first with coarse and then fine emery paper. The hilt and butt are filed and sanded as the handle is shaped.

12. Polish the blade with a medium-grit glue-up emery wheel. Polish the hilt and butt on a muslin wheel charged with polishing compound.

13. Sharpen the blade on a medium-grit hone. Always use special honing oil for all honing.

14. Polish the blade on a fine-grit glued-up emery wheel and again polish the hilt and butt.

15. Give final sharpening to the blade, using a fine-grit hone.

16. For final polishing of the blade, use a hard, polishing wheel to remove the last fine hone scratches. Give final polish to the hilt and butt and the final polish to the handle with a soft muslin wheel.

17. Make, or have made, a sheath patterned to fit the blade with a stop for the hilt so the point cannot pierce the sheath and with splines along the side to prevent cutting of the stitches. Use a keeper strap and fasteners to hold the knife in the sheath.

Bo Randall has had so many requests that he is now supplying all the various essentials needed in such home knife manufacture—from the blades themselves, which may be secured from him in different stages, up to the fully ground, sharpened, and polished steel itself, all ready for hilt and handle. Or, for two dollars, you can start with a piece of the best-obtainable knife-steel of the proper length for forging.

For a parts-and-price list, send fifteen cents to cover postage and handling to: W. D. Randall, Jr., Box 1988, Orlando, Florida 32802. Knifemaking can be a fascinating and money-saving hobby, and if you'll follow directions, you'll end up with the kind of knives I have—with which you can butcher and skin either a full-grown grizzly or a bull moose without any need to stop for re-sharpening. These are the only knives with which I've been able to accomplish either of these tasks.

KNIFE SHEATH

On my desk, I keep *Seeds-ke-dee*, which my old friend, Col. Townsend Whelen, one of the greatest woodsmen of them all, made by hand in 1916 from a Green River butcher knife. Its name is the old Indian cognomen for the historic Green River of Wyoming. The Colonel made the rugged and functional sheath at the same time. Here is how he went about it.

Taking a piece of heavy cowhide, Colonel Whelen cut it to fit the particular knife, leaving a 4½-inch-long strap at the top of one later-folded half. This strap he tapered from 1¼ inch to ¾ inch, bending it back upon itself as a belt loop

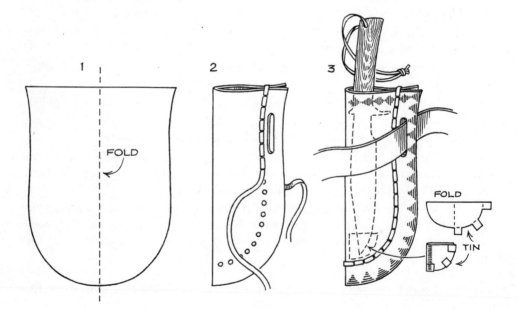

and both riveting and sewing it to the back of the sheath. The fact that all but one inch of the knife rests within the tightly clasping sheath makes any other provision against loss unnecessary.

Then my friend punched holes a quarter-inch apart all the way around both outer edges and laced the sheath together with a quarter-inch-wide strip of white rawhide, taking care to bring this flatly through the holes and around the reinforced edge of the knife holder. First, of course, he saddle-soaped the rawhide, working the lather in well, then soaked the strip in water so that, when drying and shrinking, it would tighten more snugly. The two rawhide ends he tied off by securing each beneath a couple of snugly drawn loops.

We're proving that such a simple sheath is good for at least two lifetimes.

ARROWHEADS

If there's anything that beats the fun of finding Indian arrowheads, it's making your own. Although flint is most generally thought of, other easily chipped stones such as jasper, quartzite, volcanic glass, chalcedony, and even nephrite jade were, and still can be, successfully used.

When you start with a large chunk, the first step is to break off individual flakes, arrowhead-size, by holding the larger rock edgewise on another solid surface and hitting it sharply near its edge with a sidewise twist. This will chip off thin pieces, some of which can be used for your arrowheads.

The second step is to shape each of these usable segments by chipping its edges with a sharp-pointed stone. Or, you can make your own handy tool for this work by hammering a large nail into a conveniently shaped wooden handle, then filing the head to a point. Too, if you hold your flake on a board,

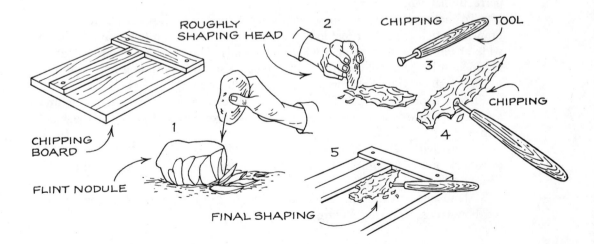

ROUGHLY SHAPING HEAD   2   CHIPPING   TOOL

3

CHIPPING

CHIPPING BOARD

1

4

FLINT NODULE

5

FINAL SHAPING

you'll discover that the work will proceed more easily. You can even provide a hold for the bit of stone you're chipping by nailing two slats at right angles on this wooden base.

Chip the flint or other stone or bit of glass roughly to the shape desired. As shown, the Indians used to vary these. The more sharply pointed arrowheads, such as I've dug up from one side of the continent to the other, were the ones used in hunting.

Finally, hold your nearly completed arrowhead firmly and flake off the last few bits by pressing down hard on it with your flaking tool. Reverse the arrowhead from time to time so as to work evenly on both sides.

BOW AND ARROWS

It is suggested that you include some steel, hunting arrowheads and a bowstring in your survival kit. You can't be expected to be as proficient with these on short notice as was the experienced American Indian, but an otherwise weaponless man should be able to get more meat with a bow and arrow than barehanded.

Well-seasoned wood is the best to use for the bow, but pick a branch or limb that is not brittle. A tree that been killed by a forest or prairie fire, especially an ash, is particularly good bow material. Other good woods are hickory, juniper, oak, white elm, cedar, ironwood, willow, birch, hemlock, and yew.

The proper individual fit for an Indian bow is often determined by holding the bow stave diagonally across the body, with one end of it clasped in the right hand at the hip and the other touching the fingers of the left hand when this is held straight out to the side, shoulder high.

The Sioux, Crow, and other western tribes generally used four-foot bows. In the East, certain tribes carried a longer bow. Ordinarily, all these bows were perfectly flat when unstrung.

To make your survival bow on the spot, take a well-seasoned yet supple branch or stick about four feet long that can be worked into a bow stave 1¼-inch wide at the center and ⅝-inch wide at the ends. The bow can be either flat or rounded. A branch, incidentally, will be more easily worked into a rounded bow.

To fashion your bow properly, start with your 1¼-inch branch and cut it off to the proper length. Then find the exact center of the remainder and mark off a space two inches wide on either side of this mid-mark for the hand grip.

Next, mark off ⅝ inch at either end. Draw a straight line from either extremity of the hand grip to the now marked ends. Draw and whittle the bow as in Figure A.

About one-half inch in from either end of the bow, make the notches for the bowstring, following Figure B.

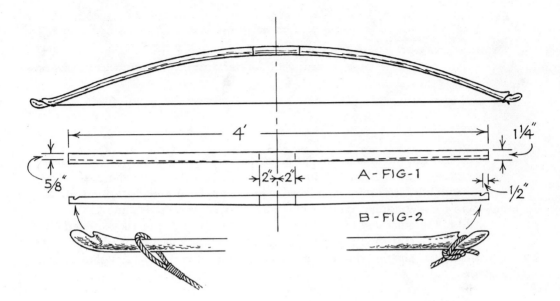

When the bow is finished, rub it all over with oil or animal fat. You'll find it will bend best the way the whittling has slightly curved it.

Although it is recommended that you carry a bowstring in your survival kit, one can be made in the field of twisted fishline or threads, nylon cord, a rawhide thong, or anything handy that is sufficiently strong.

Birch is one of the better woods to use for the arrows. To go with your Indian-type bow, these should be about two feet long. Make straight shafts of seasoned wood about 5/16-inch in diameter. Chip or whittle a nock about ¼ inch deep in the center of one end.

The feathers come next, although direction-maintaining substitutes, even wood chips, can be used instead. Using a sharp knife, split the feathers down the middle. Cut the feather in the shape indicated in Figure 3.

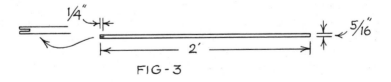

FIG-3

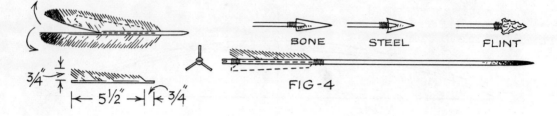

The feathers are bound to the arrow in the following manner. The first feather goes on at right angles to the nock and straight down the shaft. The second and third feathers are placed equidistant from the first. Bind all as in Figure 4, using fishline, cord, dental floss, or whatever else is handy.

Add to the other end of the arrow a tip of metal, bone, or rock—preferably flint or one of its previously considered cousins which you will be able to chip into shape. Or, simply whittle a point and harden this in the campfire. Then practice.

STONE KNIFE

The preliminary steps in making a stone knife are similar, although these Indian tools and weapons varied some in shape and were, of course, larger than arrowheads.

You can often find deer and similar antlers in the woods, especially in early winter before the porcupines and mice start to gnaw their succulencies, and a tine from one of these can be used for the hilt. Or, you can utilize a short length of birch or similar hardwood.

Just cut a blade-receiving notch in the stouter end, as shown, so that the half will fit solidly. Cement it there, with pitch made by simmering pine or spruce gum. Then bind the blade securely in place with thin strips of the inner bark from some tree such as the cedar or, better, lash it with wet sinew or rawhide.

Under survival conditions, knowledge such as this may save your life.

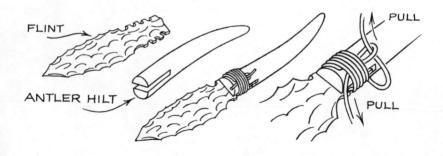

STONE SPEAR

The head of the stone spear is similarly fashioned. When the head is ready, find a straight dry sapling about four or five feet long. This should be heavy enough to balance the weight of the head.

Notch this shaft to receive the blunt end of the blade—which should be smeared with hot pine or spruce pitch to hold it in place, then securely bound with wet rawhide that, when drying, will shrink even more tightly. The Indians sometimes tied feathers to the butt of such a shaft for balance.

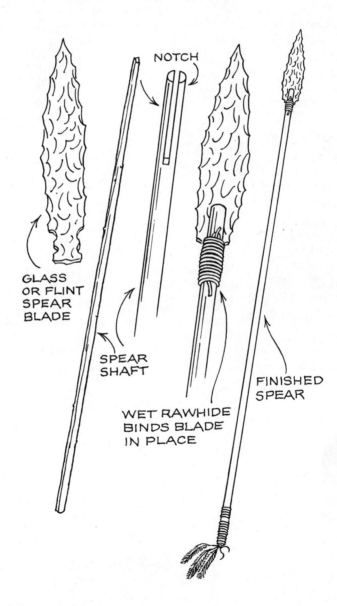

GLASS OR FLINT SPEAR BLADE

NOTCH

SPEAR SHAFT

WET RAWHIDE BINDS BLADE IN PLACE

FINISHED SPEAR

BOOMERANG

Boomerangs, made from pieces of hardwood with the curve of a parabola, come principally from three different parts of a tree. The hunting variety is cut from either a tree crotch or from near the base. The warfare type is cut near a limb. The returning kind, used primarily for play but also for securing game, comes from the angle in which the tree branches.

The boomerang, which can secure birds and small animals, is discharged by grasping it by one end, the convex edge being forward and the flat side upward. Swing it back and then sharply ahead, as shown in the drawing. With a little practice, you can become surprisingly accurate.

9

Water Supply

SOLAR WATER STILL

The same piece of plastic, which may be folded and borne in a breast pocket for shelter and other everyday uses, can save you from dying of thirst in the desert or at sea.

In the deserts of the world, with a plastic sheet six feet square, up to three pints of water a day can be extracted from a bowl-shaped cavity some 20 inches deep and 40 inches across. Place a cup, can, upturned hat, or other receptacle in the center of the hole. Anchor the plastic all the way around top of the opening with dirt or stones. Set something such as a fist-size rock in the center of the sheet so that the plastic will sag in a point directly over the container, as indicated in the illustration.

Heat from the sun shines through the plastic and is absorbed by the sand, causing the evaporation of the moisture already in the earth. The vapor is almost immediately condensed on the cooler underneath of the plastic, the

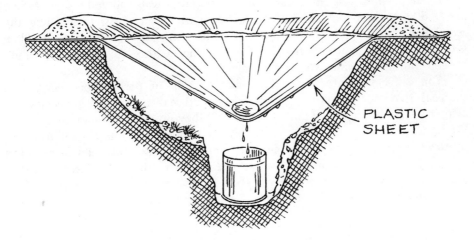

PLASTIC
SHEET

drops flowing down the underside of the steeply angled sheet and dripping into the ready container. Capillary action causes more water to be attracted to the surface of the sand to replace that which has gone, and the process will go on.

Two such stills will, when operating well, keep a man going in the desert, for even when production lessens after a day or two, it is a simple matter to move the still. Production will even continue at night at about half the daytime flow.

Varying with the condition of the soil, the amount of water you can expect to extract in twenty-four hours will be from less than a pint to three pints. But you can help the process along, particularly if you have selected a hollow or a dry wash for your location.

You'll get even more fluid by cutting cacti and other water-holding desert plants into pieces and dropping them under the plastic. The rate of output can thus be increased to nearly three times that of the sand alone. Too, even contaminated water such as urine, sea water, and radiator fluid that is not diluted with a volatile antifreeze can be purified if poured into the hole and allowed to vaporize and drip in the heat.

Sea water in the bottom of a boat, in fact, can be vaporized and condensed in pure drinkable form by this same method. Incidentally, no matter where you set up such a solar still, remove the plastic as seldom as possible, as it takes about half an hour for the air to become resaturated and the production of water to start once more.

WATER FILTER

In the tropics, you can make a handy portable water filter by first stuffing one end of a three-foot section of bamboo with clean grass, then filling the remainder of the hollow with sand. Another way to use sand as a filter is to pour water into a cloth that has been ladened with sand, allowing the fluid to seep through this into your receptacle.

You can clear water with filters such as this, or perhaps one containing charcoal from your campfire, although you should realize that such processes will neither affect any dissolved minerals, nor will they do away with any impurities. Wilderness water is polluted, as you know, by mineral and animal substance, not by the often discoloring vegetable matter such as roots and dead leaves. The aim of a self-contrived filter is to clear water by straining solid foreign matter, such as mud, from it. Then to purify, boil for five minutes at sea level and an extra minute for each additional 1,000 feet of elevation.

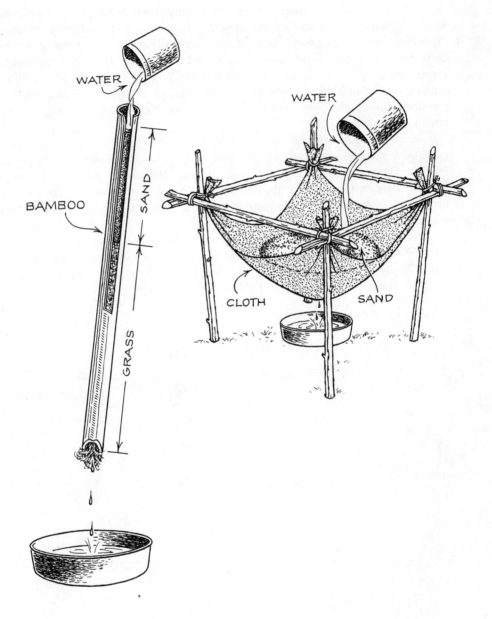

WATER

BAMBOO

SAND

GRASS

WATER

CLOTH

SAND

WATER-HOLDING BASKET

When our North American Indians hung their baskets on maple trees in the spring to catch the sweet, dripping sap, they were utilizing an ancient craft that, on this continent at least, probably preceded the art of pottery. In fact, the earliest pots in this part of the world were likely made by plastering the insides of baskets with wet clay. Today, if you're ever caught in the wilderness without a liquid-holding receptacle, and forced to depend upon your own resources for survival, an easily made coil basket could make living a lot less strenuous.

You'll need evergreen roots, perhaps spruce, for the main part of the container, plus willow bark for the wrappings and fastenings. The inner bark is used. This can be easily removed in long strands if you'll first soak the branches so as to separate the inner bark from the outer. As for the little evergreen roots, pulled up in lengthy strands, these should be soaked in warm water and the bark peeled away.

Start your basket by winding bark around the end of a spruce root. Then turn the wrapped end back upon itself and wind both in place, as indicated by the drawings. Keep on wrapping the root coil with bark, taking an occasional stitch with the same material to hold this coil in place.

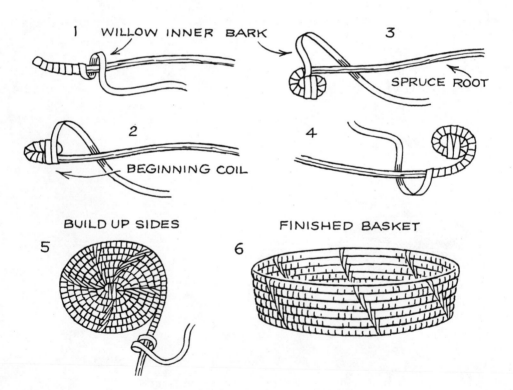

Overlap your spruce root wth a new root, binding both in place with continued wrapping, when each approaches an end. Once the flat basket bottom has reached the circumference you want, build up the rounded sides by stitching the continuing coil atop the last bottom coil. Continuing in this fashion, you can make the basket any height. Incidentally, once you become proficient in this art, you'll find that you can have the fun of forming designs with your stitching, making a more presentable product.

If you're fashioning your watertight basket at home, a big darning needle will ease the work. In the woods, you can substitute what was used by the aborigines as a snowshoe needle, made by sharpening both ends of a short length of bone or hardwood and boring a hole in its middle.

POTTERY

There are a couple of tricks to making pots similiar to those still turned out by the Pueblo, Zuñi, and Hopi Indians. First, you need to add a small amount of tempering to the clay to keep it from cracking when fired. A number of different ingredients may be used for this: crushed shells if you're by a beach or river, powdered rock such as lava, or even the remains of fired pottery.

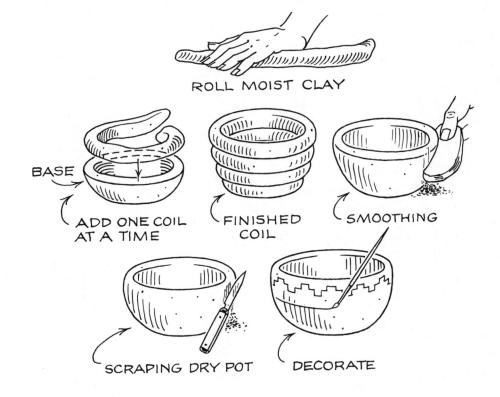

ROLL MOIST CLAY

BASE

ADD ONE COIL AT A TIME

FINISHED COIL

SMOOTHING

SCRAPING DRY POT

DECORATE

Once the clay and the temper have been screened or fingered to remove all debris such as straw, leaves, and pebbles, mix them with water to a dough-like consistency, kneading and pounding this to dispel any air pockets. Next, pat a small wad to a saucerlike base, shaping this with the pressure of the heel to your master hand.

The second secret is that the sides of the bowl are then built up, one coil at a time, with ropes of clay and temper that you roll out with the hands and palms. Finally, smooth everything with a stick. Once the pot has dried, scrape off all loose bits with your knife. The final results will be even better if you can now sandpaper everything.

In any event, the pot must be entirely dry before it is fired. One way to start this action is by warming and drying the ground with a campfire. Then set grating or a couple of iron strips over it on stones, first arranging kindling beneath. Place the pot, open mouth downward, atop the metal. Cover the entire mass with dry manure and set everything afire. Once the wood and dung have burned to ashes and the pot has slowly cooled, remove it, wipe it clean, and then rub it with oil or fat.

Or, you can fire the pot within a large can, around and on top of which a fire is allowed to burn for several hours and then cool slowly of its own accord. The clay oven you're perhaps using other times for baking bread is also eminently suitable.

10

Tools and Implements

PRIMITIVE BUILDING TOOLS

Where tools are few, as when you're throwing up a hut or log cabin pioneer-fashion in the backwoods, ingenuity flourishes. The square, even if it be but the upper back corner of an ax head, should be kept busy. The measuring implement, perhaps just a notched stick, should also be worked overtime to make the job easier.

A sharp stone, a soft-nosed cartridge, or the burned end of a stick can replace the carpenter's pencil. Any of these tied to a thong, or to a tough, flexible vine or root, will provide a compass. The butt of an ax or hatchet that has been driven into a stump becomes a backwoods anvil. A plumb line? Any lace or such with a stone tied to its end.

The builder not wishing to imitate the Leaning Tower of Pisa needs no expensive level. The bushman's plate of water will do, Or you can use a can or any flat-bottomed receptacle. The contrasting color of tea, perhaps one of the many wild brews, makes this device even more satisfactory, while the long slim bottle of fluid with its telltale air bubble is too fine for any but the very experienced.

PAN OF WATER
USED AS A LEVEL

AXE USED AS
AN ANVIL

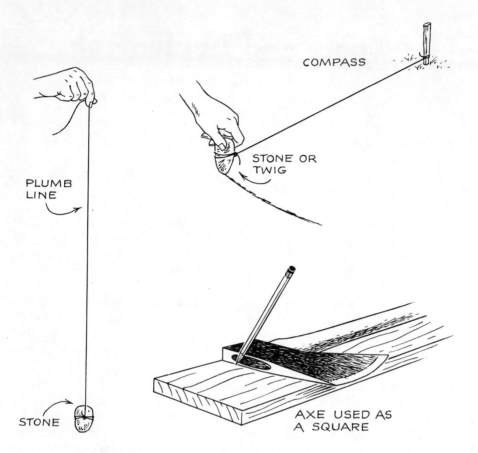

SPUD

A spud, a long piece of wood flattened on one end like a chisel, is generally used in the wilderness for driving moss or other insulative caulking between the logs of a cabin. Its softer, yielding surface grasps sphagnum moss, for instance, better than metal. A spud can be whittled from a piece of seasoned hardwood in a few minutes. About a 2-inch blade at the end of a 12-to-14-inch handle makes a handy tool for ordinary work. A malletlike piece of root can be even more convenient to use with this than the back of an ax.

TOMAHAWK

The light ax, used as a missile and as a hand tool and weapon by the Algonquians who named it and by other North American Indians, can be interestingly, and in a pinch functionally, duplicated today. Although the heads of the original tomahawks differed in shape, the type shown in the drawing can be attached to a handle with particular security. Make it from one of the previously suggested stones, work in two notches top and bottom, and continue roughly chipping the two working edges until both are sharp.

A hickory sapling will make you an especially practical handle. Shape the top of this with your knife so that a tongue of rugged bark remains, long enough to bend around the tomahawk head with enough left over to be bound securely to the helve. Before wrapping this tongue across the notches, make it more pliable and adaptable by soaking it in boiling water. You can use tough inner bark for wrappings, but wet rawhide will be far better. Crisscross it, as shown, to attach the stone head securely.

There's a trick to cutting down a tree with a tomahawk. The Indians used to build a fire around the trunk, confining its effects to the first several feet of the tree by plastering a heavy coating of mud around the trunk at waist level. As the wood blackened and charred, they hacked at it with their tomahawks until, sufficiently undercut, the forest giant toppled.

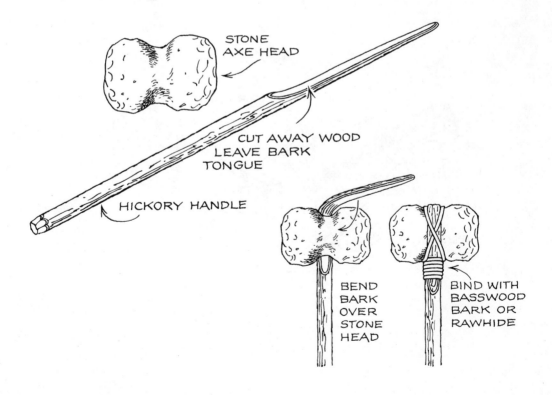

STONE
AXE HEAD

CUT AWAY WOOD
LEAVE BARK
TONGUE

HICKORY HANDLE

BEND
BARK
OVER
STONE
HEAD

BIND WITH
BASSWOOD
BARK OR
RAWHIDE

AX AND SAW GUARDS

A functional, lightweight saw guard can be made from a corresponding length of old garden hose, split lengthwise so that it can be pushed over the teeth. There it's fastened by short lengths of soft wire, twisted around both blade and guard.

An ax guard, in turn, can be easily fashioned from wood with a slot sawed in it. This can be held over the sharp edge of the ax with a loop of inner tube. Smaller rubber bands around each end of the slotted wooden piece will keep it from shifting on the ax head.

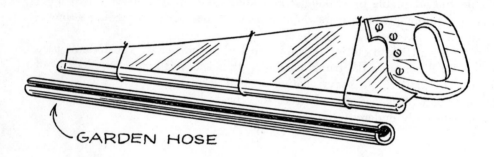

GARDEN HOSE

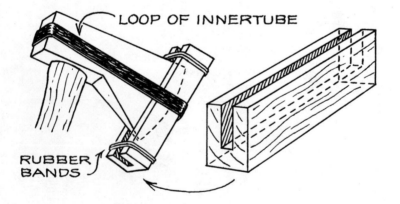

LOOP OF INNERTUBE

RUBBER BANDS

WILDERNESS BROOM

One of these will enable you to keep a neat camp. At our own Canadian log cabin in Hudson Hope, British Columbia, we find a wilderness broom of this sort unequalled for sweeping paths in the dry snow of the Far North. Although small, green, pliable birch branches, about two feet long, are our favorites, other pliant limb extremities as from ash and spruce can also be used.

A seasoned sapling, the length of an ordinary broom handle, will serve admirably to hold your wilderness broom head, especially if you notch this length of wood all the way around its lower end. Such a notch will enable you to bind on the head more securely, perhaps by winding a similar green withe— or thin, wiry spruce, hemlock, fir, tamarack, pine, or cedar root—around the brushing portion. Finally, take your knife and trim the twigs bottom and top.

A well-made broom of this type will serve for several years.

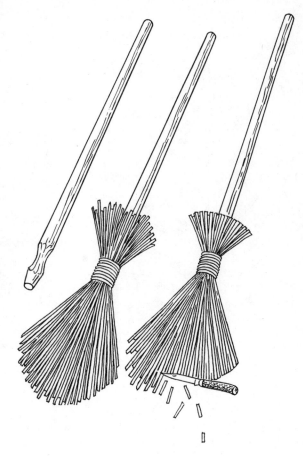

SCOURING BRUSH

The widely distributed horsetail family, *Equisetum,* was enjoyed like asparagus by Julius Caesar and his Roman cohorts. This plant is edible only when young. Later it develops poisonous aconitum tendencies. The horsetail grows in two forms, one resembling tiny fir trees and the other the highly silicious, long entities that pop apart when pulled and, in some localities, given the name of jointgrass. This latter type is also known by wilderness cooks as the scouring brush.

Our pioneer ancestors used to make a scouring brush of these horsetails by pulling up a large handful, binding them together in the middle with some handy grass or vine, and then cutting off both top and bottom evenly and neatly. Such a brush will really clean campfire soot from a frypan or kettle. The green makings grow free for the using by many of the streams where you'll most likely be preparing your wilderness meals.

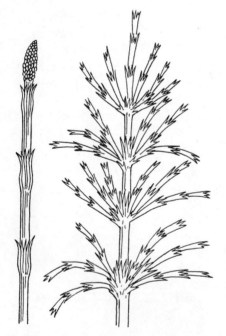

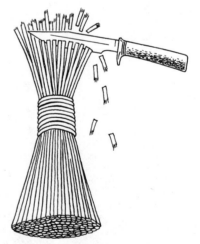

HORSETAIL OR SCOURING RUSH

11

Avoiding Getting Lost

MAGNETIC COMPASS

The compass—which along with gunpowder was one of the wonders brought from the Orient to Europe seven centuries ago by Marco Polo—was, some 4,000 years earlier, a chunk of magnetic ore suspended from a rawhide lace. You can still approximate one of these primitive compasses by first stroking an ordinary sewing needle in one direction with a piece of silk or with the pocket magnet you may have with you if you're prospecting.

The next step will be to place the thus magnetized needle where it will be free to turn. This you can accomplish a bit more easily, if now you rub the needle with oil (the small amount that can be collected by passing a thumb and forefinger over the nose and forehead is sufficient).

Then take two thin strands of grass, or perhaps a couple of threads from your clothing, and double them to form two loops in which to cradle the needle. Lower this into still water such as a tiny pool trapped by a stump or rock. If you are careful, the top of the water will bend noticeably under the needle but the surface tension will still float it. The supports may then be cautiously removed.

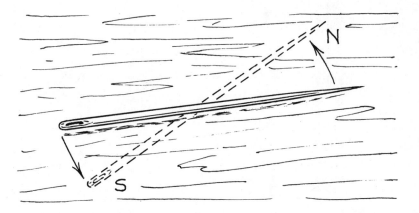

The floating needle, once freed, will turn until it is aligned with the north and south magnetic poles unless, as the case with any compass, some metal is near enough to distract it. If you have stroked the needle from the tip to the head, in the United States and Canada, the tip will point north.

SUN COMPASS

Push a short pole into the ground, making sure that it is vertical by holding a weighted string beside it. Then loop the string, lace, thong, vine, root, or whatever around the base of the pole.

Holding this taut, measure the length of the pole's present shadow. Then tie or hold a sharp stick to the line at this precise point. Draw a half circle, either starting at the tip of the present shadow or marking this point with a stake.

In the United States and Canada, the shadow of the pole will shorten until it is noon by Greenwich mean time. Then the shadow will commence lengthening again. Watch for the moment it once more meets the arc. Mark this point with a second stake.

A line, connecting the pole with a point halfway between the first and second marks, will run north and south. South, of course, will be toward the sun.

You can accomplish the same thing another way. Again sometime before midday drive a rod vertically into the ground. Mark the end of the resulting shadow with a peg or stone. Keep on so marking the shadows while they shorten, then begin lengthening again. The shortest shadow will run north and south.

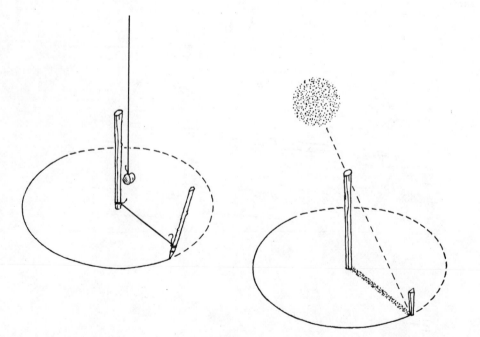

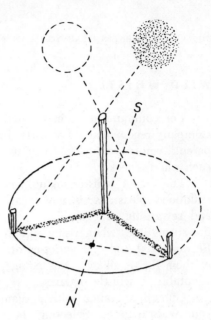

MOON COMPASS

There is an even swifter method of telling direction from shadows. All you need is moonlight or sunlight strong enough to cast a shadow. Press or drive your pole or stake into the ground as before.

Mark the top of the resulting shadow with a twig or pebble. Five or ten minutes afterward, mark the top of the new shadow. A line joining the second mark with the first will, again in the United States and Canada, point generally west.

This method is surprisingly accurate during the middle of the day. The line runs a bit south of west in the morning. Afternoons it tends somewhat north of west. During a day of travel by this method, however, these inaccuracies will average themselves out.

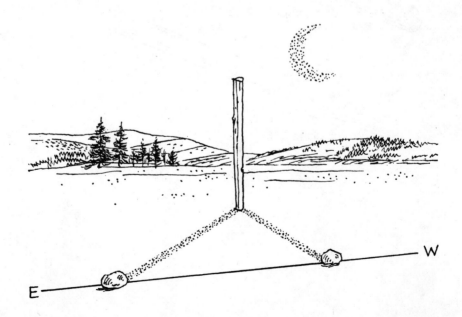

WILD WHISTLE

For communication in the wilderness, the three-century-old Hudson Bay Company recommends a whistle. In fact, a shrewd precaution taken by many parents whose youngsters play near the woods is to hang a whistle around each child's neck.

The art of whistlemaking, once numbered among the more common of childhood pleasures, is now nearly lost, but the process remains as simple and rewarding as ever. The best time to construct your wild whistle is in the springtime, when rising sap in the trees makes the bark more workable. Between 200 and 300 varieties of willow grow in the world, about one-third of them thrive all over this country—which is lucky, as willow is particularly adaptable to whistle making.

Cut off a branch with a diameter that approximates the size you want your whistle to be. Selecting the smoothest portion, make a slanting cut on one end and a square cut on the other. Approximately one inch from the latter, cut through the bark all the way around. Then cut a notch about an inch from the girdling to the slanting end.

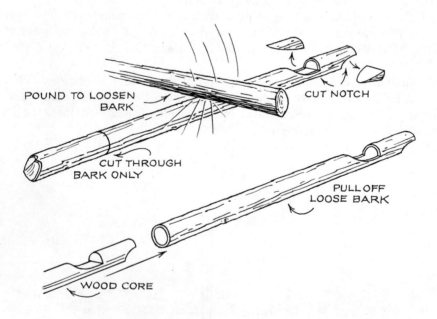

POUND TO LOOSEN BARK

CUT NOTCH

CUT THROUGH BARK ONLY

PULL OFF LOOSE BARK

WOOD CORE

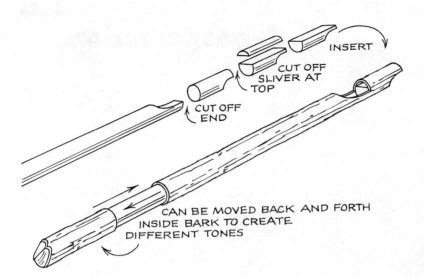

Gently pound the bark, taking care to avoid breaking it, all the way around the short piece of wood from the girdling to the slanting end. When you have done this enough, the bark will slip off like a cylinder.

Next, following the drawing, whittle the exposed wood around the notch and flatten its upper inch, from notch to square end. Slide the bark cylinder back on, and you're ready to toot. Other whistles, both smaller and larger, can be similarly made to give you a great variety of tweets.

12

Transportation

PLASTIC CANOE

When I was aching to escape the Boston rat race and take to the woods, it was my friend, Arthur C. Holman, Canadian prospector and philosopher, who first told me that Hudson Hope, British Columbia, was the most desirable bit of wilderness he'd ever seen. Here is how Art Holman, who presently lives alone in the New Brunswick woods and is as sagacious as ever, is making himself a new canoe at the cost of only about $10.

You'll need a regular canoe for a mold, but inasmuch as it will not be harmed at all by the process, you may be able to borrow one. Completely wax the whole outside so that a dose of urethane or polyurethane will not stick to it when you spray on this plastic foam one inch thick.

The outside surface of the resulting new canoe will probably be a bit rough, so sand it smooth before you lift it off. Once it has been removed from the mold, cover the inside with glass cloth and resin. Dress the outside with

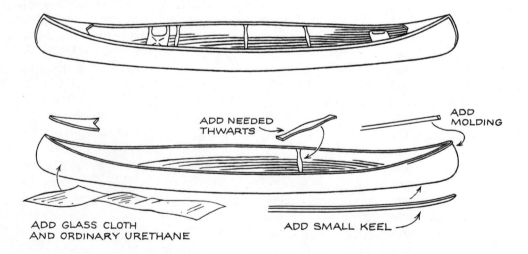

ADD NEEDED THWARTS

ADD MOLDING

ADD GLASS CLOTH AND ORDINARY URETHANE

ADD SMALL KEEL

glass cloth and ordinary urethane. Add whatever thwarts and seats are needed, plus molding for the gunwales to protect the top edge.

The finished job, in the usual small canoe, will weigh less than twenty-five pounds and will actually be much stronger than the original craft. In fact, a canoe as light as this will blow around like a autumn leaf without a small keel of an inch or so, which can be aluminum. A good idea, too, is some reinforcement at the stern if an outboard motor is to be occasionally clamped there.

With one man paddling, a weight of some 70 to 80 pounds in the bow (perhaps just a few handy rocks) will be essential, because when the canoe is unloaded, you'll have a displacement of less than half a cubic foot of water, floating about an inch in the water. With even a 200-pound man's weighing a mere 10 pounds afloat, such a light canoe is a bit tricky to get into without a weight up forward. But this is a small matter, especially when you consider ease of paddling and portaging.

RAFT

Three long logs will make, for one man, a raft that can be poled or paddled with reasonable ease. A raft for three individuals, on the other hand, should be about twelve feet long and six feet wide, depending of course on the size of the logs available. Ideally, these logs should be from twelve to fourteen inches in diameter and well matched in size so that the notches you make in them will be level once the crosspieces are driven in place.

A knife and hatchet can complete the job. An ax will make it even easier. Build the raft on two skid logs, placed so that they slope downward to the bank. Smooth these logs so that the raft timbers will lie evenly across them.

Cut two sets of slightly offset, inverted notches, as shown in the drawing, one set in the top and the other in the bottom of both ends of each log. Make each of these notches broader at the base than on the outer edge of the log, as indicated. Use a small pole with straight edges, or a taut string, to mark the notches. A three-sided wooden crosspiece, about a foot longer than the total width of the raft, is to be driven through each of the four sets of notches.

Complete the notches at the top of all of the logs. Turn the logs over and drive a three-sided crosspiece through both sets of notches on the underside of the raft. Then finish the bottom sets of notches and drive through them the other two crosspieces.

If you want and if you have the materials, you can lash together the out-jutting ends of each pair of crosspieces at either end of the raft, giving the whole structure added strength. However, when the contrivance is immersed in water, the crosspieces will ordinarily swell and tightly bind the raft together.

However, if the crosspieces are found to be fitting too loosely, wedge them with thin, boardlike pieces of wood you have split from a dry log. When the raft is in the water, these will expand, fastening the crossmembers tightly and staunchly.

To keep your feet and gear dry, you can make a deck of light poles on top of this raft. Now cut yourself a sweep, as shown in the drawing. Use a pole, however, to move the raft in shallow going.

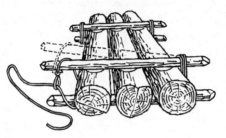

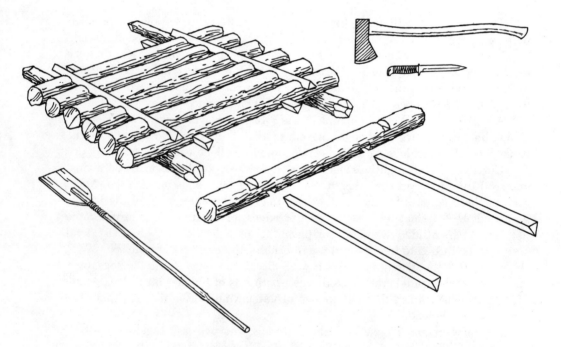

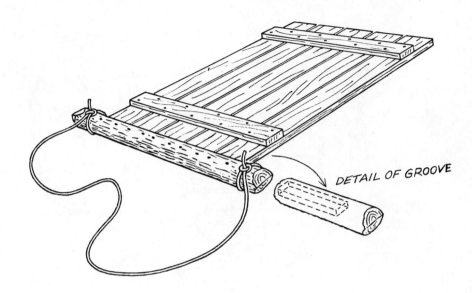

DETAIL OF GROOVE

LOGBOGGAN

When you don't have a toboggan, a logboggan can be handy in moving supplies over snow. For the front of this, pick a light, smooth log. Cut a slot in it to receive the flooring which will be several light boards, held together fore and aft by cleats across their tops. Attach a hauling rope, and you're in business.

SNOWSHOES

You'll use less energy walking on top of the snow than struggling through it. Therefore, throughout much of the winter wilderness, you should have some sort of snowshoes even if they are only light, wide evergreen boughs attached to each foot.

The oval, bear-paw snowshoe, similar to the one illustrated, will be the easiest to construct and wear and will work fine when obstructions are not too thick, as in the continental northwest. When you have to travel through thicker woods, a narrower and longer web may be necessary. You should be able to improvise either of these from actual snowshoes, or pictures thereof, that you've seen.

For the frames, cut down substantial live saplings, let them thaw in front of your campfire if necessary, and bend them into the desired shape. Strips of rawhide will make good enough webbing. In hilly going, leaving on the hair

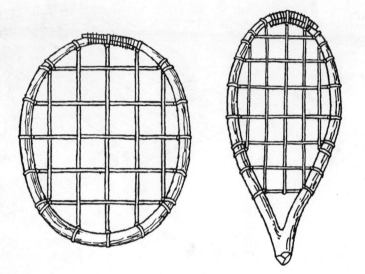

and facing it outward will help cut down on slippage. If you have wire, snare wire perhaps, string this on the frame and twist the rawhide around it.

You can also use rope in a pinch, but it has the disadvantage of stretching in cold and shrinking in slushy travel. In the first instance, you'll likely have to stop and tighten it, whereas if you don't loosen it when it's wet, it will be apt to break the frames. Rawhide is also a nuisance when the weather warms, sagging as it does when wet. The wire nucleus will do away with this trouble.

The snowshoes should be as small and as light as you can wear and still get across the snow you have to traverse. In soft going, they'll have to be larger, of course, and the webbing strung closer together.

You'll want to attach the webs so that the front of the shoe will swing up and out of the way by its own weight when the foot is raised. Even with store-purchased webs, though, some sourdoughs help themselves along in rough going by tying a rope to the front of each snowshoe and then assisting its swing with their hands.

SNOWSHOE HARNESS

In the far North the sourdough's favorite snowshoe harness is made not of rawhide, in the often elaborate complexities seen in store, but of plain, ordinary, cotton lampwicking, the same that is sold for use in coal-oil lamps. Attached to the snowshoes as shown in the drawing, this can be easily donned and detached, even when temperatures are 60° below zero. In fact, another major reason why many professional northern woodsmen prefer them is that they are less apt to harden in the cold and then chafe.

When tied, such lampwicking should be adjusted to the wearer's foot so that it will fit snugly and not loosen during walking.

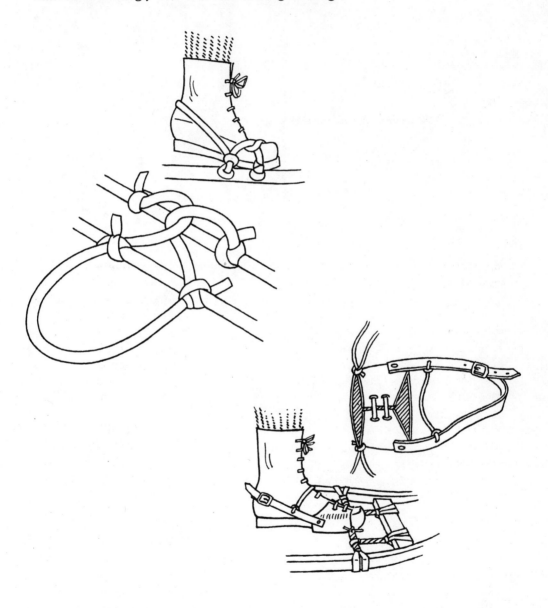